Treasure of Great Worth

A Collection of Stories, Poems, and Images
"Get MY Children Ready to Fly"

Kathy S. Mapp

Copyright 2021 Kathy S. Mapp

Book cover by Kathy Mapp with appreciation to Linda Lee for allowing me to use her artistic concept, "Children Can Fly"
All rights reserved

Published by Juania Books LLC
www.juaniabooks.com

All rights reserved

No part of this book may be reproduced, scanned or distributed in any printed, mechanical, photocopying or electronic form including information storage and retrieval systems, without prior written permission from the author or publisher. The only exception is by a reviewer, who may quote short excerpts in a review. Please do not participate in or encourage piracy of copyrighted materials in violation of the author's rights. Purchase only authorized editions.

Library of Congress Control Number 2022931566
ISBN 978-1-7339643-1-9
Printed in the United States of America
First printing 2022

This book is a work of non-fiction…

Unless otherwise identified, Scripture quotations in this publication are from the King James Version.

Scripture quotations marked (NKJV) are taken from the New King James Version, The Open Bible Edition. Copyright 1983 by Thomas Nelson Inc. Used by permission. All rights reserved.

Scripture quotations marked NET are taken from NET Bible® copyright ©1996-2017 All rights reserved. Build 30170414 by Biblical Studies Press, L.L.C.

Scripture quotations marked (Aramaic) are taken from the Holy Bible From Ancient Eastern Manuscripts 1957 by George M. Lamas. Used by permission. All rights reserved.

Scripture quotations marked NLT are taken from the Holy Bible, New Living Translation, copyright © 1996, 2004, 2015 by Tyndale House Foundation. Used by permission of Tyndale House Publishers, Inc., Carol Stream, Illinois 60188. All rights reserved.

Scripture quotations marked MSG are taken from THE MESSAGE, copyright © 1993, 2002, 2018 by Eugene H. Peterson. Used by permission of NavPress. All rights reserved. Represented by Tyndale House Publishers, Inc.

Permission has been obtained for the following:

Permission has been granted by Linda Lee of lindaleecreates.com, Redding, CA, to copy the concept of her photograph, "Children Can Fly" For my book cover.

Permission has been granted by Nathan Mapp to include his comments on the Principle Approach to education as recorded in Chapter 4.

Permission has been granted by Gretchen Hall to use the content of our interview as recorded in Chapter 9 and Chapter 8.

Permission has been granted by Dr. Nicku Kyungu Mordi to use the content of our conversation and information gathered from her life as edited for Chapter 19 and Chapter 11. End Note #5 now included in Chapter 11 and any material from any of her children's books- "to save the next generation", as stated in her permission letter.

Permission has been granted by Jenna Sartor to use her photos, words, YouTube Videos, or any other expression we have shared, in this published work.

Dedication

*Have you ever looked into the
Eyes of a newborn infant?
They can see straight to your heart.
Past the veils and shadows and
Into the love, joy and peace
That is yours to give and receive.*

CONTENTS

Dedication……………………………………………………..…..5

Contents ………………...………………………………………..6

Preface …..…..……………………………………………….…..8

Introduction……………………………………………………....12

Chapter 1 – The Serpent in the Room – Part 1……………..…14

Chapter 2 – The Serpent in the Room – Part 2……………....20

Chapter 3 - Holy Spirit in the Womb………..………….........22

Chapter 4 - Mimi's Children………………………..…………...32

Chapter 5 – The Christian Idea of the Child …...…...……..… 61

Chapter 6 - The Fruit of Our Labors of Love……………..…...64

Chapter 7 - Jenna, with 2 n's…... ..……………………….…..74

Chapter 8 - Children Who Can Fly……………….…..…….….85

Chapter 9- Jenna's Unending Progress………..……………...91

Chapter 10 – Gretchen …………………………………….…..95

Chapter 11 - Nations That Know You Not Will Come…….…...97
       To You. Nelly, Maria, Lupe, Dr. Nicku Kyungu Mordi

Chapter 12 - I Met an Angel Today and other……………....105
       Testimonies

Chapter 13 – Forever Children..112

Chapter 14 – Transference...118

Chapter 15 - Agency / Agencies...127

Chapter 16- Baby Baptism……………………………...........134

Chapter 17 – Apologetics……...138

Chapter 18 - Treasure of Great Worth 145

Appendix 1 Baby Book Example for Crafters 150

Afterword: Other Dream and Final Word 152

Bibliography…………...156

The Author…………...158

Preface

Without the following scriptures, this book would not have been written. He put His FIRE in me through His Word to spark the FIRE in you for His children. I love how Adam Clarke describes Matthew 3:11 in his New Testament with Commentary and Critical Notes, page 53:

> I indeed baptize you with water unto repentance: but he that cometh after me is mightier than I, whose shoes I am not worthy to bear: he shall baptize you with the Holy Ghost, and with FIRE.
> **With the Holy Ghost, and with *FIRE*.** That the influences of the *Spirit of God* are here designed, needs but little proof. Christ's religion was to be a spiritual religion, and was to have its seat in the *heart*. Outward precepts, however well they might *describe*, could not *produce* inward spirituality. This was the province of the Spirit of God, and of it *alone*; therefore he is represented here under the similitude of *FIRE*, because he was to *illuminate* and *invigorate* the soul, *penetrate* every part, and *assimilate* the whole to the image of the God of glory. See on **John 3:5**.
> **With *FIRE*** — και πυρι. This is wanting in E. S. (two MSS. one of the ninth, the other of the tenth century) eight others, and many *Evangelistaria*, and in some *versions* and printed *editions*; but it is found in the parallel place, **Luke 3:16**, and in the most authentic MSS. and versions. It was probably the different interpretations given of it by the fathers that caused some transcribers to leave it out of their copies.

So you see, Holy Spirit FIRE was and is misunderstood, even to the point of leaving it out entirely. I have been asked to bring it front and center.

Here are some of the scriptures that connected with me, bringing the idea to mind, that our very young children even the babes in the womb could be baptized in the FIRE of Holy Spirit and know the things of God needed to live the Kingdom life on earth.

At that very hour the disciples came up to Jesus and said, Who is greatest in the Kingdom of heaven? So Jesus called a little child and made him stand up in the midst of them, and he said, Truly I say to you, unless you change and become like little children, you shall not enter into the kingdom of heaven. Whoever therefore will humble himself like this little child, shall be great in the kingdom of heaven. And he who will welcome one like this little child, in my name, welcomes me.
Matthew 18:1-5 Aramaic

Then little children were brought to Him that He might put His hands on them and pray, but the disciples rebuked them. But Jesus said, "Let the little children come to Me, and do not forbid them; for of such is the kingdom of heaven." And He laid His hands on them and departed from there.
Matthew 19:13-15 NKJV

This next one I discovered while writing this book, so I made it mine, so to speak. I call it the Kathy Mapp translation: It is bringing together in thought, the Aramaic (Ancient Eastern Manuscripts) for the tone; The KJV for the wording and Strong's Concordance for the definition of words.

Luke 10:21. *At that very hour, Jesus rejoiced* **(G21; jumped for joy, exalt(ed))** *in the Holy Spirit and said, I thank You, Father, Lord of heaven and earth, because You did hide these things from the wise and men of understanding and revealed them to babes.* **(G3516; not speaking, i.e., an infant.)**

David understood the vastness of God, the Holy Spirit:

Whither shall I go from thy spirit? Or whither shall I flee from thy presence? If I ascend up into heaven, thou art there: If I make my bed in hell, behold, thou art there. If I take the wings of the morning, And dwell in the uttermost parts of the sea; Even there shall thy hand lead me, And thy right hand shall hold me. If I say, Surely the darkness shall cover me; Even the night shall be light about me. Yea, the darkness hideth not from thee; But the night shineth as the day: The darkness and the light are both alike to thee. For thou hast possessed my reins: Thou hast covered me in my mother's womb. I will praise thee; for I am fearfully and wonderfully made: Marvelous are thy works; And that my soul knoweth right well. My substance was not hid from thee, when I was made in secret, and curiously wrought in the lowest parts of the earth. Thine eyes did see my substance, yet being unperfect; And in thy book all my members were written, which in continuance were fashioned, when as yet there was none of them. How precious also are thy thoughts unto me, O God! How great is the sum of them! If I should count them, they are more in number than the sand: When I awake, I am still with thee. ***(Psalm 139:7-18)***.

This scripture really rocked my world when He opened my understanding:

And Mary arose in those days, and went into the hill country with haste, into a city of Juda; and entered into the house of Zacharias, and saluted Elisabeth. And it came to pass, that, ***when Elisabeth heard the salutation of Mary, the babe leaped in her womb; and Elisabeth was filled with the Holy Ghost: and she spake out with a loud voice,*** *and said, Blessed art thou among women, and blessed is the fruit of thy womb. And whence is this to me, that the mother of my Lord should come to me? For, lo, as soon as the voice of thy salutation sounded in mine ears, the babe leaped in my womb for joy.* ***(Luke 1:39-44)***.

Notice in Acts 2, when Peter was filled with the Holy Spirit power he spoke with a loud voice. A voice of authority from the Father, in Holy Spirit power to break through old mindsets establishing relationship with their Savior and ministry for the Kingdom.

In an amazing colliding of circumstances, Holy Spirit opened another scripture that points even more closely to Holy Spirit FIRE in the unborn and the tiny infant. Luke 18:15 "Then they also brought infants to Him that He might touch them; but when the disciples saw it, they rebuked them. But Jesus called them to Him and said, 'Let the little children come to Me, and do not forbid them; for of such is the kingdom of God'" **(Luke 18:15-16 NKJV)**.

According to Strong's Concordance, the word infants in this scripture is **G1025 – "of uncertain affinity; an infant (properly, unborn) literally or figuratively – babe, (young) child, infant."** Only Luke uses this word to describe the children that came to Jesus. And he wrote from eye witness accounts of the people surrounding Jesus. There were six accounts in the book of Luke and none in Matthew, Mark, and John.

They did not want Jesus to be bothered with the children, but Jesus said to let them come and He touched them. No water baptism necessary. Just a touch can start a FIRE of the Holy Spirit. A word started the Holy Spirit FIRE in Elizabeth and John. I guess the water in the womb might count as the Water that comes with the Blood.
(1 John 5:6)

An additional scripture was given to me by the Lord during my morning devotionals:

> *I've come to start FIRE on the earth – How I wish it were blazing right now! I've come to change everything, turn everything right side up – how I long for it to be finished! Do you think I came to smooth things over and make everything nice? Not so. I've come to disrupt and confront.*
> *(Luke 12:49-51 MSG).*

Introduction

This publication comes with a FIRE of God attached. He has awakened me and instructed me through many sources, that now is the time to renew and rewrite. He has called me to "Protect the Children."

Writing is what I understand He means for me to do because in the years past He sent three individuals to tell me "There are books in you to write." Until now that seemed preposterous. Well, so did it seem preposterous to begin having children at the age of 40.

Preposterous is His way with me. So preposterous it will be. I am definitely not an author in my own right, but to HIM, I am who He wants me to be.

The underlying theme will be how God is in every detail of our lives from the beginning. And the beginning of our lives in God is not when we are born into the earth. Our lives began in God the very moment HE thought of us. He has kept every single one of us hidden in Christ from the very beginning.

Doesn't He say in Ephesians 1, and in John 1, that we were in the WORD and the WORD was with God and the WORD was God, and everything that was and is created is created by the WORD? Our true identity has been and always will be who we are in Christ, the Living WORD of God.

Which brings us to the emphasis of the stories in this book, knowing our identity in Christ even as a baby. And I have discovered that what is needed to truly know our identity in Christ is the FIRE of God, which is demonstrated in Mary's encounter with Elizabeth. This might hold the key for anointing the babes in the womb with the FIRE of God.

So the hope in the writing of this book is to encourage every parent, guardian, teacher, and grandparent to begin at an early age to instruct children in the loving nature of God and the WORD of God and impart the FIRE of God.

As these encounters with God and His WORD and His Holy Spirit begin to come alive in our children's lives, they will know who they are in Christ, their purpose and their destiny. The soil of the heart is the most important thing to begin with.

Teachers call this "soil softening" the heart to receive the seed of the WORD so it produces 30-60-100-fold fruit, which means, the children bring true Kingdom thinking and living into the earth.

Just look around. Our world cannot teach them the truths they need to know. We ourselves must know the truth that sets us free so we can be the salt and the light needed for our world and they can learn from us how to find the salt and light the Lord has put in them, which prepares them to be ignited by the FIRE of Holy Spirit.

So, let's begin. I truly hope you enjoy the journey. And that you discover new truth to encourage you on the way.

Chapter 1 - The Serpent in the Room – Part 1

I woke up one morning in a dream. I was alert enough to remember and write it down. It was on 7/12/2021;

I saw a round dome shaped object – it was a kettle making tea and it had spots on it.

I remember thinking I had to get the spots off. Somehow, they represented to me "unclean, sin."

I heard the voice of the Lord say: "No time to clean it. Protect the children. There are 2 ways:"

    1. "I had help and they were kept safe" (this spoke of the past).
    2. "There are a few who can help me keep them safe and we work together" (this speaks of now).

I looked up the meaning of tea kettle in dreams or visions. On one website it meant renewal, rebirth, new beginnings and spiritual supernatural sources – transferring my fears to faith in God.

It combines the powers of FIRE and water. (For me God is a consuming Fire, and water represents the Holy Spirit power in the Word and cleansing of the WORD.)

A kettle just coming to boil suggests that a project or plan is about to come to fruition. In a dream it means we need to accelerate a process of learning and growth. It can be a laborious work but a creative work.

Biblically, it was used to prepare the peace offering. Hot means handle a matter carefully.

Another piece of the puzzle I now have regarding the kettle of tea refers to the spots. The Lord showed me a stream flowing out of sight. In that stream was every guilt or shame I ever experienced or would experience. Jesus washed it away in the "cleansing flow." These are the words He said to me: "My spots are washed away in the cleansing flow. So! Protect the children."

There is an enemy – a constant battle.

In the dream, the kettle had to be continuously heated to keep the children safe. The heated tea kettle was key to their safety. Next, I would need the help of a few others working together.

As I pondered this message I wondered how, and with what, I had to act quickly to protect the children. That's how the thoughts formed into an actual plan to finally write the book He said He had put in me.

I have spent years thinking and writing in a journal what I have now written on the following pages. What I hope to present in my personal experience is an example of how God can intervene in the life of a Christian who has been duped by the Enemy of God. Does the Enemy know something we (meaning born again Christians) don't know about our children?

Remember in the Old Testament, in Genesis 3:15, the Lord God cursed the serpent saying the Seed of the woman would crush or bruise his head and the serpent would only bruise the heal of the Seed of the woman.

The serpent didn't know who nor when The Seed was coming into this world so he killed as many Hebrew baby boys throughout history as he could, and was still defeated at the Cross.

So, if that was the only Seed that was to be the problem why is the serpent still killing our babies through abortion, child pornography, slave labor, sex trade, and vain philosophies, and probably much, much more?

DOES THE ENEMY OF GOD KNOW SOMETHING WE, THE BELIEVERS DON'T?

I can't speak for all of history's treatment of children, but they have gotten the short end of the stick, and not only from the enemy of God working in the minds and hearts of the unbelievers, but even the believers have been deceived.

INNOCENCE is one of the disputed areas. Innocence means freedom from guilt or sin. Many if not most Christians believe all of Adams children are born in sin and the major mainline Christians believe the Bible tells them so. Well, I have a little trouble with the finality of that.

If I consider Psalm 139, how God knew David, formed him and knew everything about him even before he was formed in his mother's womb, wouldn't God have formed David with innocence? How precious God's thoughts were toward him! It seems from God's perspective David was much loved. Now, when David did sin with Bathsheba, it did not change God's mind about David. He was still the "Apple of God's eye," meaning God has him in the center of His sight, and he is His delight.

In Psalm 51:5, David says He was formed in iniquity, in his mother's womb; and in sin did his mother conceive him, but this was only after the incident with Bathsheba. Peter did the same thing to Jesus after Jesus filled Peter's boat to overflowing with fish, he says, "depart from me for I am a sinful man." Obedience and love are important to God. Seeing one's self through the lens of guilt and shame seems to be the standard for believers and nonbelievers even today, but God sees His children through the lens of love. We tend to see the worst in ourselves.

Jesus also sees His children through the lens of Love. He said, "Let the children come to me," and "of such is the kingdom of God."

Children are humble, forgiving, and joyful. Babies and children are innocent, free from evil intentions, with a simplicity of heart, and the enemy of God is stealing "the innocence" of our babies and our children away from us.

We have MISSED THE MARK. And doesn't Sin mean MISSING THE MARK?

There are many ministries out there to rescue our teens, children and babies, but what if we began from the very beginning of the desire for a child that rises in our heart, to declare who they are from God's perspective?

That's what I have written about, using the few examples from my life. I bet you have many more you could add to mine. We must begin declaring over our babies who they are from God's perspective, because the enemy is going to be ready to take them out. We have been given by God, who and what we need to speak into the earth and change the trajectory of loss and death to gain and life for our children.

The zeal of the Lord shall perform it through us. This generation and the next, and however long it will be before the Kingdom comes in fullness. Let's get it right from the beginning so we don't have so much cleanup to do.

The first part of the book tells what I did to keep the children, my children, safe. Other than continually reinforcing they were fearfully and wonderfully made, filled with God purpose and gifts, and loved beyond measure, I taught them PRINCIPLES, which I will expand on in the next chapters.

I now believe the curriculum He chose for my children was His Holy Spirit FIRE that was needed first in my life. I needed a renewed mind, so I was led into a particular philosophy of education called American Christian Education. Using the Foundation for American Christian

Education curriculum.

The bottom line of this curriculum is that it teaches that everything begins with God and their identity in God is formed in their heart. The life they live out into the civil arena of community, church, and nation, and world is taught governmentally. The Providential history of America, when understood, brings wisdom to respond to the needs of their community, and then nation, from God's perspective. In much of my son's reasoning, I began to see wisdom and wondered if there might be a statesman in that little boy.

If you believe the Kingdom of God is here now and is coming in fullness this is something your child will need to know, and our children from two generations ago at least don't have a clue. I'm one of those past generations. Public schools and churches stopped teaching children what the founding fathers knew that enabled them to prepare covenants to bring order to the lives of this young nation and their own identity in Christ.

Also, somehow our identity in Christ was stolen along the way and it MUST be restored first and foremost.

The next part of the book will be what I am doing in my sphere of influence to protect the children. I have shared with young mothers my understanding of the importance of knowing their identity in Christ, how fearfully and wonderfully made both they and their children are. They are the apple of His eye and loved beyond measure.

I've also shared the curriculum to help them gain a philosophy of education that prepares them to lead and rule in the realms of civilization, such as government, education, business, health, media, entertainment, and religion.

Now I must find the open doors to bring the Holy Spirit FIRE into the lives of the young and even unborn.

This next generation is already overcome with cultural chaos that had not yet surfaced in my generation. We must get ahead of this, and it will take the wisdom of God. Seek Him! He will answer. The next step is up to you. Are you called by God to be His FIRE in the earth?

What can you do to Protect the Children?

Chapter 2 – A Serpent in the Room – Part 2

In this chapter let's look at the scriptures about children from Adam and Eve until the present day.

God put enmity between the serpent and the woman from the beginning of time. The scripture says the woman's Seed will bruise the serpent's head and the serpent's seed shall bruise His heel. In this scripture the word bruised used by Strong's is H#7779

> *Bruise #7779 - a primitive root; properly, to gape, i.e., snap at; figuratively, to overwhelm: -- break, bruise, cover.* **Genesis 3:15**

Up until Jesus came, Satan was doing all he could do to eliminate the children of God, particularly the babies. Now, Jesus has come as a baby, just like humanity, and Satan was defeated by Jesus at the cross when He rose again. Death, which is the wage of sin, could not keep Him.

We are still in the crossfire of Satan and the woman, even now as children are born into the saving grace of God. Children have angels looking over them. I believe this can only be the age of innocence, because they have not had the ability to choose to remain in the grace of God or choose to go outside of the cleansing flow of God's grace.
One of the prophets of old spoke of the water that flowed from the throne of God which was for the healing of the nations, and I think

this flow has the same properties of the Grace of God as the flow of the Blood of Jesus from the cross.

God is our protector, forever on our side, forever keeping us. And in the keeping, we respond with thanksgiving and gratitude by bringing to the earth all that Jesus died for us to have.

When will the bruising end? How will the bruising end? Will it be the Seed of woman that brings the battle to an end and the kingdom to the earth in fullness?

Jesus the Seed, has given His Seed, His authority and power of Holy Spirit and Heavenly Hosts, to wrap this thing up. Babes come fully equipped with ears to hear and eyes to see. These are the ones Jesus is referring to when he tells His disciples to let the children come to Him, because of such is the kingdom of God.

What is truly possible when you believe? It only takes the faith of a mustard seed. One of the smallest seeds in the plant kingdom. Mountains crumble and fall into the sea. A little child can accomplish this even now.

Get ready world, here come the most amazing children ever born into the earth – a band of brothers and sisters that are unstoppable in all ways as they unite in all their diversity together to reconcile all creation to the maker of All.

Chapter 3 - Holy Spirit in the Womb

I want to share something with you about a conversation I had with a friend of mine today.

I told her I'm writing a book about protecting Children and I'm stuck. There's something I can't see and I want to see it. So she shared with me something the Lord has opened up for her in her writing. She read it to me: "But I will come to you shortly, if the Lord will, and will know, not the speech of them which are puffed up, but the power. For the kingdom of God is not in word, but in power" **(1 Corinthians 4:19-20).**

I looked up the meaning of "word" in that scripture in Strong's Concordance: **"'word,' logos G3056 from G3004;** something said (including the thought); by implication, a topic (subject of discourse), also reasoning (the mental faculty) or motive; by extension, a computation; specially, (with the article in John) the Divine Expression (i.e. Christ):--account, cause, communication, X concerning, doctrine, fame, X have to do, intent, matter, mouth, preaching, question, reason, + reckon, remove, say(-ing), shew, X speaker, speech, talk, thing, + none of these things move me, tidings, treatise, utterance, word, work."

Then I looked up the word for **"power"- "G1411 dunamis from G1410;** force (literally or figuratively); specially, miraculous power (usually by implication, a miracle itself):--ability, abundance, meaning, might(-ily, -y, -y deed), (worker of) miracle(-s), power, strength, violence, mighty (wonderful) work."

So "word" seems to imply in this location of scripture that the words the teachers are bringing to the Corinthian church must be measured against the power they hold. For the kingdom comes in power – Holy Spirit power.

Before Jesus began His ministry, John the Baptist said something about the baptism the people would receive through Jesus that we seem to have missed and need desperately. In **Matthew 3:11** He says, "I baptize you with water, but after me comes One who…will baptize you with the Holy Spirit and with FIRE."

The missing ingredient is FIRE.

When Jesus sent the disciples out, he gave them power over the enemy to heal and deliver. These will be the signs that follow the word spoken and believed.

Jesus assured His disciples power had been given to Him and He now gives it to them, so go. Everything you have heard from me and seen, do.

A little later He told them to wait for the promise of the Father which will come to them in a little while. And after He had been crucified and risen, He sent this dunamis power in the form of tongues of FIRE on their head and power in their heart, mind and soul at Pentecost as written in Acts 1 and 2.

Dunamis power is more than words, preaching, utterances and reasoning, it is Who Jesus sent to empower us to fulfill the great commission. Dunamis power is a person, Holy Spirit.

Could it be that the laying on of hands on pregnant mothers to receive Holy Spirit and FIRE could empower them and their babies against the deceptions of the enemy of God from the womb? Could we transfer Holy Spirit FIRE as Jesus did to Elizabeth and John while John was still in Elizabeth's womb?

I know this sounds radical, but our battle for our children is radical. Satan has known our children are what the Kingdom of God is made up of, at least when Jesus held up a child and said, "of such is the kingdom of God," if not before.

Christians have missed it for millennia. We have said that they are not innocent, that they are in sin, for all have sinned. Well, I think Satan laughs at our legalism and takes their lives in the womb, at birth, and at every juncture along life's path.

There are many amazing ministries reaching out to save and deliver babies, children, youth and young adults, but God has told me to protect the children. That is not the same thing as saving them. Only God can protect them and he is clear on that. There is only one scripture in Strong's Concordance that has the word protect and it has a suffix - protection. It is used in Deuteronomy 32 in a mocking way.

God is mocking His children for thinking the false gods could help them and protect them. He is telling them there is no other god but The Lord God who can protect them. So, that being said, it is not mere words, but dunamis power, God power, that protects the babes.

I'm reading and I've heard and I am still hearing about all these ministries reaching out to save and rescue our children from the sex industry, slave labor, pornography, Marxism, critical theories, etc., and how the enemy of God is stealing their minds and their faith. They grew up in AWANA, Navigators, memorized scriptures, recited the catechism, were baptized in water, professed faith in Jesus, yet they are easy game for the enemy.

What if we did something in the beginning of their lives, and they were born with a confidence in their identity in Christ and His identity in them. And there would be nothing anyone could say that would take that away or any power greater than the Power/FIRE POWER in them that could overtake them.

So I asked myself, "What made my relationship with Jesus real, solid, powerful?" I asked my husband, "What made your relationship with Jesus solid, untouchable by vain reasoning?" For both of us it was the

Baptism in the Holy Spirit as an adult that brought both of us back to the Lord.

Both of us were brought up in a Christian family that mostly practiced their faith. Sunday school, joining the church, Bible studies etc. What made both our faith strong and untouchable by the enemy was the Baptism in the Holy Spirit FIRE as an adult.

My husband said he could finally understand the word of God, and it was alive. For me it was this and so much more. I was hungry for the scriptures. I couldn't read it fast enough. I was like someone who was starving and a plate of food was put in front of me. And not only that, but I experienced Holy Spirit FIRE, on my head, in my language and in song and a peace that was unknown to me until then.

Holy Spirit is the missing ingredient for a life lived in victorious faith. Only recently did I see this connection to a life lived in victory because of the gift of Holy Spirit and FIRE. Jesus gave us an example in the book of Luke, when Mary goes to visit her cousin Elizabeth, who is in her 6th month of pregnancy with John the Baptist. The scriptures say that when Mary entered the room the sound of her voice caused the baby in Elizabeth's womb to leap and Elizabeth was filled with the Holy Spirit. BINGO!

So if Elizabeth was filled, wouldn't it be possible to believe that John was too?

That will be my next line of reasoning and research.

I know many people believe babies are not innocent. Well, the enemy just laughs at us Christians when we say that, because he must know something we don't, and loves that we don't get it because he is doing everything possible to steal their innocence. You get it? He's stealing their innocence – something we, Christians keep saying they don't have!

He either kills them in the womb or steals them when they get out. Why? If they are not innocent, would he need to steal his own? Think about it.

We have really missed it, and we had better not continue missing it. This generation and the ones that are coming need every life prepared by God for us. I have grandchildren, and friends that have children on the way. We need whatever God has put in each one for our and their generation. They have been prepared by God before the foundation of the world with abilities and gifts that will be needed in our world, and we who are already in our world know nothing of what is needed. Look at the condition of the world around us. God is sending help from the sanctuary, His gift to us, children.

The scripture that started this discussion said Kingdom comes by dunamis – power, not word, alone.

So let's lay hands on the babies and provide the authority that Jesus has given to them before they are born. Let's lay hands on them in the womb and get them baptized in the Holy Spirit and FIRE. Jesus gave us the example for such a thing, through His encounter in Mary's womb causing Elizabeth to get filled with the Spirit and John to leap in the womb.

The ministries that exist are still needed for the previous generations. They need to be rescued, but Jesus told me to protect, not rescue, and this is what I have come to as a way to protect the children. Let's do what Jesus did even while in the womb. We have His authority and His example, so let's be about our Father's business and really protect our children.

Power

How important is power when protecting something or someone? It's at the top of the list. King David did his exploits as a mighty warrior in the power of God. He gave praise to God for His power. Yet he was the greatest worshipper known. Worship and praise go hand in hand with the power of God to live victoriously.

> *"Wherefore David blessed the LORD before all the congregation: and David said, Blessed be thou, LORD God of Israel our father, for ever and ever. Thine, O LORD, is the*

greatness, and the power, and the glory, and the victory, and the majesty: for all that is in the heaven and in the earth is thine; thine is the kingdom, O LORD, and thou art exalted as head above all. Both riches and honour come of thee, and thou reignest over all; and in thine hand is power and might; and in thine hand it is to make great, and to give strength unto all" **(1 Chronicles 29:10-12)**.

John, when he baptized Jesus at the beginning of His ministry, said of Jesus,

I indeed baptize you with water unto repentance: but he that cometh after me is mightier than I, whose shoes I am not worthy to bear: he shall baptize you with the Holy Ghost, and with FIRE: And Jesus, when he was baptized, went up straightway out of the water: and, lo, the heavens were opened unto him, and he saw the Spirit of God descending like a dove, and lighting upon him: and lo a voice from heaven, saying, This is my beloved Son, in whom I am well pleased **(Matthew 3:11, 16-17)**.

At the end of Jesus's ministry, Jesus spoke to his disciples and prayed for them. In **Luke 24:29** he said, "And, behold, I send the promise of my Father upon you: but tarry ye in the city of Jerusalem, until ye be endued with power from on high."

And when they received the power from on high it was FIRE: "And there appeared unto them cloven tongues like as of FIRE, and it sat upon each of them. And they were all filled with the Holy Ghost, and began to speak with other tongues, as the Spirit gave them utterance" **(Acts 2:3-4)**.

Then Paul wrote to the Corinthian church about the Kingdom. He said, "For the Kingdom of God is not just a lot of talk; it is living by God's power" **(1 Corinthians 4:20 NLT)**.

How do we receive this FIRE power, and then once we receive it, how do we keep the FIRE burning? Just like David did, with praise and worship. The New Testament scripture says God is going to restore the Tabernacle of worship in the end time. Why? That is the power we need. It is FULL of Holy Spirit FIRE power.

There are children being taught to rely totally on God. Their life becomes worship to God. Just living it out day by day. Children that are taught to trust God in all circumstances, always looking to Him, will not need protection. They are literally covered with the grace and Glory of God and nothing contrary to Gods will or purpose can enter into their heart, mind, or space.

Caution- Strange Fire

This morning as I thought about how this new understanding – baptizing babies in the womb in the Holy Spirit and "FIRE" of God to protect them – could actually happen in the present reality of the church world, with all their doctrinal rules and denominational traditions, a cautionary thought arose in my mind: "Strange Fire." I remembered a story in the Old Testament about strange fire, but couldn't remember the details. So I looked it up. I found it in **Leviticus 10:1** and **Numbers 3 and 26**.

Aaron's sons, priests of the Most High God, put "Strange Fire" on the altar of incense. As I thought about it, I began to realize that the fire, itself wasn't strange, but became "Strange" before God when they put it on strange incense.

God's instructions in **Exodus 30:34-38** were very clear about the compounding of oil used for the incense and use of all elements and every priest called to the worship of God. The oil was only to be made according to the compounding instructions of the apothecary and only on those things used in holy worship.

What was the result of bringing the Fire of the Anointing before The Lord, on the prayers of His Children through the Priests that ministered before Him, and now through the Great High Priest after the order of Melchizedek? Christ, in the FIRE power of the Holy Spirit, breaks the yoke of every disease, every sin, and every sickness. Everything that is in service to The Lord of All must be touched by the Holy Anointing that comes before The Lord. Even Jesus described what that FIRE power anointing does and who has that anointing in **Luke 4: 18-19**:

> *The Spirit of the Lord is upon me, Because he hath anointed me to preach the gospel to the poor; He hath sent me to heal the brokenhearted, to preach deliverance to the captives, And recovering of sight to the blind, To set at liberty them that are bruised, To preach the acceptable year of the Lord.*

Another interesting detail about the incense altar where this Holy FIRE was burned is that it was the only alter in the heavenly temple and that FIRE was put on the prayers of the Saints to accomplish the Will of God on the earth. It is thrown onto the earth just before the seven trumpets sound in **Revelation 8:1-4**.

So when God told me to protect the children, and that there are only a few that can help, I am now thinking those few that can help are those that know they have "The anointing Fire of God" – That power of Holy Spirit that can bring the intercession before God, through Christ, our Great intercessor.

Any false or fake fire will never accomplish what is needed in this hour. Those babies that are coming have already received, before the foundation of the world, the works they will do. Providence has determined their appointed time, and it is now.

We must baptize them in the FIRE of the anointing that breaks the yoke. And by "We," I mean those who know their identity in Christ as "FIRE."

He showed me my identity as FIRE in a church wide activation many years ago. The pastor asked us to reflect on **2 Corinthians 3:18**. And asked us to ask the Lord how He wanted to reflect Himself in us. He showed me this man on FIRE. This meant that He saw me as the FIRE seen in the eyes of the Ancient of days and coming from under his outstretched arms. Also, with hair of white wool like the image in Daniel and the Revelation.

If that's YOU, then you are called to pray for the FIRE of Holy Spirit to enter into the womb of the pregnant mothers and the newly born. They have been created with end time purpose. They are going to fly for God. So we must get them ready.

But for the lost and stolen, those who have no hope nor power on their side that they know of, I know they do have someone on their side. He is a mighty warrior and He is for them. Lauren Daigle has a mighty song for the lost and stolen:

Rescue by Lauren Daigle
https://www.azlyrics.com/lyrics/laurendaigle/rescue.html

> *You are not hidden*
> *There's never been a moment*
> *You were forgotten*
> *You are not hopeless*
> *Though you have been broken*
> *Your innocence stolen*
> *I hear you whisper underneath your breath*
> *I hear your SOS, your SOS*
> *I will send out an army to find you*
> *In the middle of the darkest night*
> *It's true, I will rescue you*
> *There is no distance*
> *That cannot be covered*
> *Over and over*
> *You're not defenseless*
> *I'll be your shelter*
> *I'll be your armor*
> *I hear you whisper underneath your breath*
> *I hear your SOS, your SOS*
> *I will send out an army to find you*
> *In the middle of the darkest night*
> *It's true, I will rescue you*
> *I will never stop marching to reach you*
> *In the middle of the hardest fight*
> *It's true, I will rescue you*
> *I hear the whisper underneath your breath*

I hear you whisper, you have nothing left
I will send out an army to find you
In the middle of the darkest night
It's true, I will rescue you
I will never stop marching to reach you
In the middle of the hardest fight
It's true, I will rescue you
Oh, I will rescue you

If there are so many Christians in the world why are there so many lost and stolen children? What happened? Did we only have the word and no power to live it? YES.

Fox News Headline, Wednesday, September 29, 2021, 10:12AM – "A warning on the days and times children are most like to get kidnapped"

This says it all. They are able to forecast kidnapping. God help us!

I grew up in a home that called themselves Christian and I belonged to a church that did not recognize the Holy Spirit calling to me. They said it was hormones. As I said earlier, I was already saved, but had no understanding of what that meant, nor power to live out of the clutches of the world. I did not know Jesus loved me, really loved me, and that how I saw myself was not even close to how He saw me. And even then He knew my name.

Here's to the children and the babies that have no voice for themselves, that they know of. I am sending out an SOS. Others are actually looking for you and they will find you. Hold on. God is on your side and He always has been, but your eyes have been blinded to the truth that He is for you. He loves you, He loves you, He loves you. He knows your name and He's calling out to you.

You have been told how worthless, bad, ugly, stupid, weak, and of no value you are, and all of that is a BIG FAT LIE.

So hold on to hope, help is on the way. God LOVES YOU MORE THAN YOU KNOW.

Chapter 4 - Mimi's Children

"Mimi" is the name my grandchildren have given me, and when this book began as a seedling in my mind I pictured myself writing to their generation and the ones to come, so I originally titled my book "Mimi's Children." But as my story unfolded it became a much larger story. So, the title "Mimi's Children" was relocated to a chapter that it more clearly introduced, my own children. But I digress.

There I stood in the parking lot of the small church in Conway, FL. All the children taking the fine arts elective in our home school group met together in this little church until 3:00 pm. But this wasn't like the other Wednesday gatherings in many ways.

As I was on my way to the school a news bulletin interrupted our local radio station. A prisoner from the Orange County Prison Facility had escaped. Then instructions were given regarding safety and how to report sighting information to the local police. The church was very near the prison facility.

After the broadcast I was fearful about leaving our children at the church, but I took them on to the church anyway and as I was returning to my car I was praying for God's protection over all the children. Suddenly everything changed. I don't know if I went somewhere or if the Glory of God came to my location.

It was a presence of blinding light, weighty and something else that brought tears. I don't think I spoke, but I thought, "where am I, and what is this light?" and then I heard a voice:

"Anything that enters MY Glory that is contrary to MY will or purpose will either flee or be changed. MY Glory fills the whole earth."

Then I was back in the parking lot surrounded by other moms asking if I was alright. I couldn't talk for a while. All I could do was cry. Our son's best friend's mom stayed with me until I recovered. I told her what happened.

I knew then that God was protecting our children. So how am I to protect them for Him? Something I have learned along the road of faith is that I am a new creation in Christ Jesus and I am to be His Ambassador to bring His reconciliation. It is His will, strength, plan, power, etc. He equips me to do His will.

The very first way He led me to bring protection is by reminding me of the schooling He brought me into kicking and screaming, so to speak. I will include the leading ideas of this curriculum later in this chapter.

Now to the story of our children Nathan Russell Mapp and Mary Elizabeth Mapp. They each have their individual story. As Jesus came as a baby, in the flesh as a first fruit, so come all babies. They are a Word in the Mind of God and then a spoken Word. Spoken into existence through the woman and the seed of man. But make no mistake, it is the will of God that brings each one.

Nathan had complications, which required a time in Arnold Palmer Neonatal ICU. The nurses said he was determined to go home. They said that because of the way he responded to treatment. And it wasn't long until his wish and ours came true. He was released from the hospital and we began parenting.

Mary was born almost two years later. By now, I'm 42 years old, but the pregnancy and delivery were without incident. She had an overnight stay, and home she came.

I have many pictures of their beginning life in our home and their acceptance of each other as a member of our family. Sometimes I think pictures say more than words could ever accomplish.

Their young life together and our lives as parents was a very rich and rewarding time, but this was new territory for me and I was on a fast track to learn how to be a good mom and John, a good dad.

When they were really small, we began introducing them to the God of all creation, who loved them more than we possibly could. We took them to church and had them baptized, just like our parents did for us.

But God wanted more. He began to lead us to include more instruction into their lives at home and then with others during the week. First it was only a few days in a Moms Day Out program, where I taught. Then it was a Christian preschool program. Their experiences as small children were out of the home, as well as in the home. We added good nutrition, prayer at evening meals together, Bible stories at bed time, plus lots of outside play; but that was only the beginning of God's desire for our children and for us.

In the first part of my dream, He was speaking of our children's lives. He said, "I had help and they were kept safe." It was during the first years of their lives that we were called to home school, but it took me three years to say yes. I was the teacher and John was the principal, so to speak. He worked out of the home five days a week and I retired from the design industry to be a full-time teacher, mother, etc.

As I prepared to teach what I am about to write I literally had to break through an old mind-set. I was angry and stubborn and finally I had to yield, and I cried, because I died to that willful way of thinking. Training for reigning was what this was all about. The FIRE of the Holy Spirit was in the purging of the old and refining of the light of illumination that was in the new mind of Christ for the education of our children. And not only ours, but all who put their trust in Christ.

This came to me as a very important reason we taught our children the principles of the American Christians. There are many curriculums out there for training and teaching Christian thinking, which leads to Christian leadership, but the missing ingredient is applying the principle of self-government and Christian character to the covenant that this nation is governed by.

As Christians we are in covenant with our Creator God through the finished work of His Son at the cross. He planned and accomplished through the pilgrims and the Founding Fathers His purpose for this nation. The documents they prepared for this nation, The Declaration of Independence, the Constitution and the Bill of Rights, reveal the needed character and understanding of a government of Liberty.

This is the covenant we have with God and each other, founded on the principles of the Bible. The Preamble to the Declaration contains the entire desire of this American government, in relationship with its people and their God in a single inspiring passage:

> *We hold these truths to be self-evident, that all men are created equal, that they are endowed by their Creator with certain unalienable Rights, that among these are Life, Liberty and the pursuit of Happiness.—That to secure these rights, Governments are instituted among Men, deriving their just powers from the consent of the governed,—That whenever any Form of Government becomes destructive of these ends, it is the Right of the People to alter or to abolish it, and to institute new Government, laying its foundation on such principles and organizing its powers in such form, as to them shall seem most likely to effect their Safety and Happiness.*
> From constitutioncenter.org an essay by Jeffrey Rosen and David Rubinstein.

Do you see the part, "endowed by their creator with inalienable rights?" That is a very important part of knowledge that is essential for each child to know that what governs this country, governs their heart and lives. They are connected.

Each child has gifts that cannot be transferred to another that they are to bring to their generation. This is the missing piece in Christian education that needs to be taught. It is what they are prepared to understand, but sometimes it requires a breakthrough in the mindset of a Christian to think governmentally.

They need to think internal to external. What the person is made of ripples out into their actions and thinking in their environment. Leaders are raised up. They reveal their gifts and abilities to rule by the way they live their lives. They are someone you want to follow, not someone you are told you will follow or else. The rule of an American Christian will yield to the covenant of the nation, which is founded by God for us.

One man over all is not the model of American Christian government. It is the rule of many, voluntarily uniting in thought and action to accomplish what is best for the family, community, nation, or world in which they have been appointed to govern.

Our nation was founded, through the loss of many lives, to separate us from monarchical rule. One ruling over all, lording it over, not serving, as is the Christian model. We are a Constitutional republic, which means representational government, ruled by many.

The Federal government, which is to have the highest rule, was to be used only in case local government could not resolve a matter, or when it was necessary to join together to defend. Life, liberty, safety, and pursuit of happiness was the goal. Civil government has levels of responsibility and most of the responsibility was to be in the hands of the local government, not the Federal government.

The American approach to government is incompatible with socialism, which limits the individual and nation by making creativity, initiative or wealth, common to all without acknowledging the fact that the creativity of the one is indeed their intellectual property, and the fruit of that intellectual property is theirs to distribute as they will, not as the government wills.

Children taught the effects and affects of American Christian government as ruled by the covenants of the land, the Constitution and the Preamble of the Declaration of Independence as shown above, will continue to lead our nation in the liberty which they have received. Our Scriptures even say, "Stand fast in the liberty where with Christ has made us free, and be not entangled again with the yoke of bondage" **(Galatians 5:1)**.

Teaching the principles of the American Christian education to our children teaches them to reason with a wisdom that is from above, which this generation is in great need of; but every generation is always in great need of the wisdom from above, and that's the way our Creator created each generation to live – a life sought after HIM.

Look around – what do you see, what do you hear? Do you have eyes to see and ears to hear? Our liberties are being stolen right from under our Christian noses. So what is the solution? Is there more than one solution?

I say there is more than one but for a solution to be a real solution it must contain the serious knowledge of God, of self, of initiative and creativity, a servant heart, and courage to stand against all that would steal any of the liberties we have in Christ and the covenant that this nation was formed under.

We must teach this generation, and the next, and the next, and however many there are until God's kingdom comes in fullness to the earth. If the foundations (of this nation) are destroyed, what can the righteous do? **Psalm 11:3**.

And the Christian foundations of this nation are being stolen every day.

I would like to share a prayer I prayed for our nation after my children had finished their secondary education and were beginning their individual lives. That they would begin to apply the principles they learned in school to their everyday lives was my prayer for them. It was December 2010.

Here is my prayer:

*Lord, as Hezekiah, the king of Judah was recorded as saying in **2 Kings 20:1**, he asked You for healing and You healed him and gave him 15 more years to rule.*

He asked You, and You did it.

I ask You; "Give us our nation for Your righteousness sake." Restore truth and divine principles of just gain to our economy, liberty to speak and to own property.

Restore productivity and industry to our land. Hear our prayers to elect leaders that will tear down the idols of power that hook us and bring us to greed.

Remove those leaders that destroy Your sovereign rule in our lives and our founding documents, the Declaration of Independence and Constitution, and Bill of Rights.

Restore our rights to use and apply the individual gifts You have given us to lead, preserve and heal our land.

Restore Your throne in the hearts of your Children of every age.

Hear our prayer and have mercy on us.

Forgive our sin and slothful living of life. We have been asleep and have not watched and prayed as we needed to do and the enemy has stolen our liberties. Like the disciples in the garden, we did not watch and pray with You for even one hour. We fell asleep and our land and liberty has been steadily stolen.

Have mercy on us.

Jesus, You came to take back what the enemy had stolen from us, our identity, and from God, the worship of His children.

In Your name, Lord Jesus, we take back the voice of righteous justice, mercy and love for You and our nation.

We desire to love Our neighbor and we love YOU.

GOD HELP US. AMEN

As I mentioned before, in all my years of education I never was taught that all subjects and wisdom begin, end, and are consummated in Christ. Nor that I would be needed for any great overarching purpose of being able to keep the liberties I have in Christ and that this nation has offered in its founding documents, that others have lived and died for me to have and to keep.

Here is a statement from a well-respected master teacher of American Christian History and Government I would like to share with you.

> *Our nation is not in trouble because of the aggressive activity of socialists, liberals, communists, one-worlders, trilateralists, [wokeism, critical theories,] world bankers, etc. - it is this way because of the failure of American Christians to **remember** and **value**, the Christian history of their nation and the Biblical principles of their government and their failure to value what it cost to produce the freedoms they take for granted.*
>
> *When one knows something of what is going on governmentally – the abuses of our system, local, state and national – it is very easy to become convinced that the <u>negative forces</u> are the **aggressor** and the cause of our problems; but the contrary is true – <u>they are not but filling the places</u> which should have been **occupied by those understanding Biblical principles of government and economics.** Those we call the **offenders** are merely filling the places of leadership in all fields of endeavor, which have been given them by the **default of the Christians.** This has been going on for over a hundred years; is it any wonder that Biblical principles of government, economics and education*

> *are not in control in our country? (Verna M. Hall, 1980)*

As Christians, we often forget it is a covenant we have with God given to us through the blood of Christ, a blood covenant. Abraham received a blood covenant promise from God. A blood covenant is one that can never be broken between equals or rulers. We are covenantal in our relationship, like a marriage covenant. It's governmental! And it includes a Promised Land.

James Rose has noted that a covenant is a coming together of two or more to do, or to forbear an act, sealed with the blood of the sin offering animals, later the Lamb of God, and followed by the promises of God received by man from the perfect sacrifice and obedience of the Lamb.

Now that I've shown you Verna Hall's quote, I would like to introduce another bold statement from a man named Hugo Grotius, 1654.

He was significantly influenced by the idea that the sovereignty of the nations originates in the people, not in the kings by God's will (referring to the divine right of kings). The people agree to confer such authority to their authorities, including the kings. This was thinking that surfaced in the beginning of the 16th century.

This mindset was a part of the mindset of our nation's founders and writers of the covenants – the Constitution and the Declaration of Independence that united us as a nation separate from Great Britain.

This statement ripples out the effects of living a self-governed life as a child. Remember, Jesus says to come to Him as a child, and of this is the Kingdom of God; a little child.

Hugo Grotius:

> *He knows not how to rule a kingdom, that cannot manage a province; nor can he wield a province that cannot order a city; nor he order a city, that knows not how to regulate a*

village; nor he a Village, that cannot guide a family; nor can that man govern well a family that knows not how to govern himself; neither can any govern himself unless his reason be lord, and will and appetite her vessels; nor can reason rule unless herself be ruled by God and (wholly) be obedient to Him.

The outward flow of self-government: **INTERNAL > EXTERNAL**

The ripple effect of self-government goes out from ourselves to our family and then into the community. On my way to Travelers Rest South Carolina, one morning, my mind was racing with thoughts that matched up with some of my conversation earlier that morning. I realized I had better write it down.

As I was waking that morning, I heard #110. Quickly I thought this is a Psalm. Yes, it is, and a mighty Psalm. It sums up all the major points that are covered in this writing. Please consider reading Adam Clarke's commentary on this Psalm. It is solid meat. Vol. III, pp. 580-587.

My heart rejoiced to read how important the government of God is to His Children of all ages. In verse #3 It is a government of liberty where the will chooses whom it will serve and whom it will let rule over it. God alone will rule in our hearts and through our lives. Adam Clarke calls the Children of God - "the cheerfully beneficent people. They hear His call, come freely, stay willingly, act Nobly, live purely and obey cheerfully." Clarke's Commentary vol. III, p. 582.

Also, the reference to the womb of the morning and the dew of thy youth, Clarke says of The Lord and of us:

> *As the human nature of our Lord was begotten by the creative energy of God in the womb, of the virgin; so the followers of God are born, not of blood, nor of the will of the flesh, but by the Divine Spirit...all genuine Christians (Children of God) may be fully compared to 'dew', for the following reasons:*
> 1. *They had (and have) their origin from heaven*

2. *They fructified the earth*
3. *They were (and are) innumerable*
4. *They were (and are) diffused over the earth*
5. *They came (come) from the beginning, salvation*
6. *They came from the east and moved west (westward move of Christianity)."*

-Clarke's Commentary, vol. III pp. 582-583.

This is so encouraging to me. This many years later I have confirmation of the huge importance of the Children of God understanding the Government of God for their lives and the many lives they will encounter along the way.

Also, Adam Clarke's description of "will" brings clarity and joy to the need for living freely in the perfect will of God. How important it is to voluntarily choose someone or something. When it becomes forced, it is no longer from the will of the individual but the will of the one forcing. We become machines governed by the one who makes the machine go.

If you look around today you might notice the number of Children of God seem to be declining. In Faith I say **Isaiah 9: 6-7** shall be and are being performed, because the will of the Lord shall perform His Word, which is His government is on the increase, by His zeal.

And those of His children who have forgotten who they are have received encouraging instruction: "Put away the old life with all its practices and put on the new life which is RENEWED in KNOWLEDGE after the pattern in which it was originally created" **(Colossians 3: 9b-10, Aramaic).**

Come Holy Spirit. Send Your FIRE. Ignite our children's and our own hearts to Your Will. Your kingdom is coming in Power, and Your children must be ready to fly.

It's time for pictures to introduce our children and to break up the explanation of the first part of the dream in which God said, "I had help and they were kept safe."

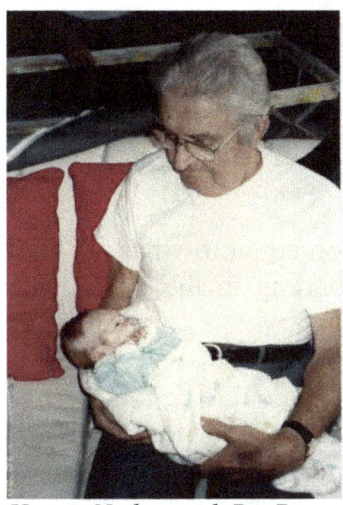 

Here is Nathan with PopPop *Nathan is one year old*
Just home from the hospital

Nathan is our first child. The story of his life requires faith beyond my understanding at the time of his birth. We had been to the Doctor and, yes, I was pregnant. It was early in the first trimester so we had not told anyone.

One day, I think it was in the 4th week I began to feel strange. And as Preposterous as this is going to sound to some, I felt life leave my body.

I called the Doctor, and my husband to come get me for a doctor visit, and I called the women that had been praying for us, asking them to pray. I can't remember all the details about the doctor visit, other than it was a Friday, but it was determined that I was to return to the office on Monday and if my hormone count had risen the baby was still alive and growing.

Sometime during the following days as we waited and prayed, I felt the life return. Sure enough, my hormone count had risen into the eleven hundreds. Our baby was alive. For some this would be considered preposterous. How can I feel life come and go within myself? Well, I don't know how, but I just Know. This is for me the evidence of the power of prayer in the plans of Gods providence.

Eight months later Nathan, named because Nathan means gift of God and he surely was that to us, arrived with some complications, but alive and well. His story from this point includes some of the most amazing doctors and nurses.

I would compare their care and determination equal to what we have experienced from our medical teams responding to the COVID-19 epidemic.

It was later confirmed by a geneticist that she could see that he had some trauma in the fourth week that prevented one of the blood vessels in the umbilical cord from being created. Nathan only had two and the "normal" number is three.

So, here's a question I have had since his "resurrection" in my womb. This will be another preposterous part of his story, our story, but is he already living a kingdom life on the earth if it is appointed for man to die once?

In the natural he died and in the natural he was raised again, or was it also supernatural? And if that is so for Nathan, is it also true for Lazarus in the Bible and all those who have been resurrected in this age? Just curious!

Maybe one of the readers of this story has an answer. I would love to hear it if you do.

Ok, then comes the news that I am indeed pregnant again – just some months later. This child has a story as well. We found out the baby was a girl. What shall we name her?

We looked at all the family names, but nothing popped. Then I remembered the scripture of confirmation of the promise that I would be married. It was in **Luke 1:45**: "Blessed is she who believed, for there will be a fulfillment of those things which were told her from the Lord."

This scripture was given to Elizabeth in her old age as she was pregnant with John, to be called the Baptist, as Mary, the mother of Jesus came into the room where she was staying.

So, Mary Elizabeth Mapp, the baby's name.

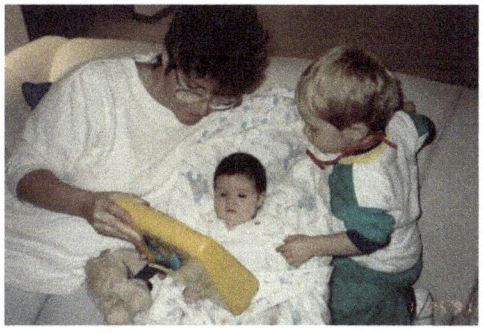

*Here is Mary just weeks after her birth.
Nathan beginning to accept his sister*

Her arrival was without incident. So another chapter of life begins for my husband and me.

 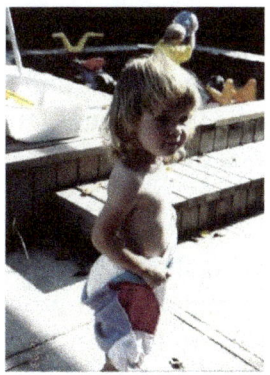

Mary at one year old.   *Mary at two years old*

As I mentioned earlier, I did not have the understanding when our children were born, that even babies can know the things of God and respond in their own way to Him. It was in the rearing of these two precious gifts of God that we began to see how they were able to understand and have a relationship with Jesus, the WORD of God.

Here's one of those times. When Nathan was two or three, very young, I was frustrated about something and said something in anger to him. I quickly realized what I had done so I said, "Nathan, can you forgive mommy for saying angry words to you? I'm very sorry, please forgive mommy."

He turned to me and said, "Jesus, please forgive mommy." And off he went to play. I don't know if you get the amazingness of that. Nathan was talking to Jesus as if THEY WERE FRIENDS. He was a small child, the very one that was resurrected in my womb. So, I ask you, how did he know that it was Jesus that would require my repentance? Preposterous, yes, but it is becoming less and less so. Preposterous will become natural and glorious with all these experiences of a life lived for God and through the study of our life as Americans in the 21st century in relationship with Jesus to bring our nation to God, to kingdom living and not only our nation, but all nations.

Each generation has the responsibility to carry on the kingdom witness to the next generation. And each nation has its own story of true relationship with the Living WORD for their generation. We are not the same. The diversity and individuality are in everyone and every nation, and choosing to unite together in the diversity and individuality is an honor and privilege. It does not require force from any government, it requires respect of each other's choosing, within the guidelines of scripture or truth. We must teach this to our children or it will end.

What I hope to show you through the life of our natural birth children is how the principles that provide a base, or spring board, for living in liberty while a young child prepare the mind and heart for life beyond themselves, beyond their family, beyond their community, beyond their nation, and into their world.

Nathan was in the ICU at Arnold Palmer at first. We brought tapes of us talking to him, telling him how much we loved him, who God says he is, that he is wonderfully made, and lots of songs and stories. The nurses would play the tapes for him throughout the day. I just know they were angels.

When we brought him home, I was determined to tell him what I thought his Heavenly Father would want him to know. I believed God had put in Nathan everything he would need to live a strong, happy and healthy life.

I played cassettes of Bible stories, Bible scripture put to music, lullabies, and we would tell him how precious he was to us and to Jesus. At night we would softly play Christian lullabies until he went to sleep.

As he grew older, he was fascinated with the mirrors – that he could see himself. We would tell him who he was as he looked at himself and he would laugh at himself and reach to touch himself in the mirror. When he could walk, he would walk up to the mirror and touch it with a smile.

Sometimes we would play in front of the mirror and I would constantly be telling him about himself. Who God says he is and that Jesus loved him and we loved him.

I remember how troubled I was when he began to have nightmares. We did some research about that and found that as babies grow their brains begin to grow more and more synapses to connect the lobes and allow the neurons to fire in the brain. This is the beginning of going from concrete thinking to abstract thinking. Sometimes their thoughts can be "dark" or cause nightmares. At those times I would read the Psalms over him. He would respond to God's word and quiet down.

When his little sister was born, we did the same for her. She was shy about looking at herself in the mirror at first. But we told her how beautiful she was, and that we loved her, and that Jesus loved her more.

Mary liked the stories but didn't want us to sing. It was funny because she later was the singer. She would sing "Jesus loves Me" while she was playing outside. I painted a picture of her doing just that in our back yard when she was three or four.

John and I believed it was very important in these formative years to only put good in the eyesight and hearing. There was a song that I sang called "Be careful little eyes and ears and mouth." The words told the children to be careful what they hear, what they see and what they say. The Father up above is looking down with love.

There were shows that were just right for little ears and eyes, like "Mr. Roger's Neighborhood." And later it was the "Adventures in Odyssey" series. There were always questions concerning what was okay to watch on TV or videos.

Another important part of their beginning was prayer. We prayed over our food. We prayed every morning, and at night when they went to bed. Sometimes our friends would even feel led to pray over them. We had a friend that would come and clean our house and when she cleaned, while they were napping, she would go pray over them.

I was a Sunday school teacher so I would share my stories and crafts with them.

I believe this daily input of who God is, who He says they are and how He has created a world for them that is good and a life of purpose for them prepared them to incorporate the teaching of the principles.

Also, the important thing was to love God and to know He loves them and Jesus loves them, and the golden rule to do unto others as you would have them do to you.

We were able to surround them with what we believed would be the best for them. In as many ways as we knew how, we taught them about Jesus and the life He has for them. We taught the Proverbs to them to help them gain wisdom even from an early age.

I recently discovered, while doing my own Bible study, that the eastern regions of the world teach proverbs to their children when they are small, and not just Christians. The book I was reading was on the Oriental thinking behind the stories in the gospels, particularly the parables and the proverbs. it was written by an eastern Indian Hindu who had converted to Christianity. He said, "all children learn the Proverbs because they teach wisdom for life, even though most children are not Christian."

Something I began to question concerning my children, was, "Like Elizabeth and Sarah of the Old Testament, do my children have a purpose or destiny for God that is for such a time as this, since they were born at a later time in my life?" I believe in the providence of God to create and provide for His creation through His children, and He told His creation to take dominion over the earth He had created for them.

His time is eternal and His creation is still being revealed. He has put the works that we should do in us before the foundation of the world to be revealed providentially in chronos time. There is so much more to know and so much more to discover about our God and ourselves, our world and each other.

Another Principle we taught was Christian character. Character is defined – a mark made by cutting, or the particular qualities impressed by nature or habit on a person that distinguishes him from others.

The Christian character – virtue – is strength, moral goodness, practice of initiative, industry from a sincere love of God; and His

Word is true virtue.

Voluntary obedience, was something I learned about when I taught K-4 at a Christian school. The Lord said to me that in obedience is blessing. Blessings flow out of obedience. I used to tell my students, "If you want a blessing from God, obey your parents." It's automatic.

What they learned as young children blossoms into an ability to reason rightly as an adult, the very principles that formed this nation and made it great. The founding documents only work if the people understand how to use them to make this nation great and keep it great. It begins in the heart of the individual and ripples out into the family, community, nation and world.

There is a 1779 quote by Samuel Adams that speaks to the importance of Christian Character:

> *"A general Dissolution of principles and manners will more surely overthrow the liberties of America than the whole force of the common enemy. While the people are virtuous, they cannot be subdued; but when once they lose their virtue, they will be ready to surrender their liberties to the first external or internal invader…If virtue and knowledge are diffused among the people, they will never be enslaved. This will be their great security."*

With Christian character- the virtues of Christ, we will be able to walk as children of light in a perverse generation.

This will be the beginning of correcting the wrongs in the running of our nation governmentally, economically, educationally, socially, and individually.

Teaching Christian character by the Word of God in the power of the Holy Spirit FIRE must be done in every generation. God must be brought back into the education of our children, so the leadership they provide in their generation strengthens their nation.
Each nation must make that decision as families raise their children and they become the leaders of their nation in their generation

I watched my children grow into their strengths and use them in their families and community. Now as I have become motivated by God and challenged with the need to prepare the next generation to reason and relate with sound reason that will return our nation to righteousness, I am more purposefully taking every opportunity with my grandchildren to teach Godly Character.

This is really moving into the governmental arena, but this is where we are failing to stand strong and keep our liberties. For too long we have given away the very liberties me fought to have. I have taken a giant leap to believe it is because we have not instructed with the Holy Spirit FIRE which is also a zeal, the same Zeal of God that will continue to grow the government of God on the earth **(Isaiah 9)**.

Here are pictures of our children from their childhood. Many of the things they experienced, they experienced together, but the takeaway for each was very different as they became adults. This is the example of the individuality of each child, individuality in diversity.

Karate Kids

Silver Springs, FL

Nathan reading to Mary.

Home School learning

Home school learning

Who God had created them to be was becoming who they were. Their personality, their intellect, their abilities and gifts – we call that individuality and intellectual property. So can you see the problem if the government wants to rule the life of a child through education? They would be forming their thoughts instead of allowing the creativity and intelligence they have been born with to be produced in them. We will lose the liberty in which we have been created to thrive if education without the knowledge of God is forced on our children by government controls.

The wisdom and knowledge of God is unending. Once a door swings open and we discover the contents, or we go through and learn to accept into our lives what we have found, boom, another door swings open. An unending supply. That is what the principles have opened in my belief system, and what I have tried to teach my birth children and spiritual children.

Be assured there is a force out there that would want to limit all aspects of life – particularly each person's individuality. If you are allowed to think for yourself and create, the possibilities would be endless for our world and the world to come.

We must start when they are newborn to tell them who they are in Christ. It's never too soon. I have shared all the ways we taught our children about their identity in Christ. This prepares them for the principles that ripple out into their participation in their generation.

If we can teach our children principles of individuality, Christian character, conscience as the most sacred property, self-government, voluntary union, just to name a few, our nation will return to the liberty in which it was founded and fought for and our children will confidently take their place in this world.

This is not a political statement – this is about government. Government that begins in the heart of the child and ripples out into their home, community, nation and world. It is the Liberty, which God has given to us in Christ in each one of us. The word government asks the question, "Who will you allow to rule over you? Will you let Christ rule in your heart, and then from that relationship prepare you to rule rightly in your home, family, community, nation and world?"

Now that we have looked at Individuality, Self-Government, and Christian Character we are ready to bring the fourth Principle into focus, which is conscience is the most sacred of all property.

This is one of the most important and probably the least understood principles. It is a treasure that Jesus purges with His FIRE.-

> *"How much more shall the blood of Christ, who through the eternal Spirit offered himself without spot to God, purge your conscience from dead works to serve the living God."*
> ***(Hebrews 9:14 KJV)***

The founding documents have this as one of the most important Principles that separate us from other nations. Our Declaration of Independence, Constitution and Bill of Rights stand on this truth.

Here is how the other 3 Principles form around this one.

1. *The Principle of Individuality - is reflected in the diversity of each child of God. Their character and conscience are uniquely formed by their relationship with The Lord Jesus. Their quality of the certainty of their identity in Christ determined in their heart from a child reveals itself in the government they will allow to rule over them and as they are a part of the government that rules.*
2. *The Principle of Self-Government expands as God's law and Love are accepted and obeyed in the individual heart. Local self-governing homes, churches, and communities are maintained by individuals that govern with the Wisdom from Above.*
3. *American Christian Character, in the case of individuals living in the United States of America express a God-governed nature with qualities of character as those in the founding fathers, faith, courage, initiative, industry and brotherly love. Only those whose heart is ruled by the one True God and life has been refined by conflict within and without can maintain a Christian Republic.*
4. *Conscience is the most sacred of all property. As God's property, individuals have a God given right (a just claim) to the most sacred of all property – Liberty of Conscience and of Consent. Its effect externally is conscientious stewardship of private property, with its fruits, is protected by just, written laws established by the consent of the governed.*

Quote from James Madison, "Property" 1792:

"...In the former sense, a man's land, or merchandise, or money, is called his property. In the latter sense, a man has a property in his opinions and the free communication of them. He has a property of peculiar value in his religious opinions, and in the profession and practice, dictated by them...He has an equal property in the free use of his faculties, and free choice of the objects on which to employ them.

In a word, as a man is said to have a right to his property, he may be equally said to have a property in his rights. Where an excess of power prevails, property of no sort is duly respected. No man is safe in his opinions, his person, his faculties, or his possessions. Where there is an excess of liberty the effect is the same...Government is instituted to protect property of every sort...This being the end of government...Conscience is the most sacred of all property; other property depending in part of positive law, the exercise of that being a natural and unalienable right...A just security to property is not afforded by that government, under which unequal taxes oppress one species of property and reward another species..."

As my husband and I were talking about this quote I asked him if he thought we could be worse off today and he thought there is a good chance that is true. The appearing of wokeism, Critical Social Justice Theory, redistribution of wealth, etc., makes the ability to keep this American Christian Republic, even as a Christian, seem impossible. We are as grasshoppers in our own eyes.

Few of the women I have met have the understanding of American Christian Principles themselves nor are they teaching them to their children. This is where the enemy of the Liberty we have in Christ is winning.

Since that time, I have seen our liberties threatened or stolen. I am seeing this book as sounding the alarm to protect our children and the liberties they have in Christ. The character they have acquired through all the difficulties have prepared them to stop this train wreck.

They have been called for such a time as this. Their acute awareness of their relationship with Jesus makes them ready to turn things around. We must make ready for them to stand on our shoulders by having a level of understanding ourselves as parents, guardians and teachers and we must bring the FIRE of the Holy Spirit into the individual lives of our children. They already have planted in them what God has determined for them to bring to their generation.

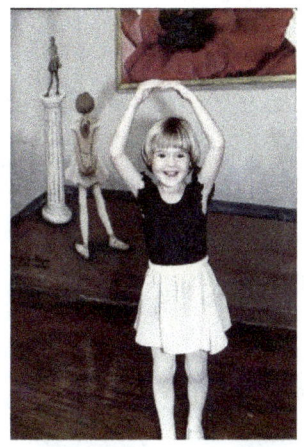

Mary struggled with this curriculum. It was too regimented, too legalistic, too many rules. She wanted to know where the liberty was that I kept talking about. I remember I had that same thought often times when surrounded by other parent teachers and Master teachers.

So the challenge became for me, to find the joy. Joy was given by God to Christ because of righteousness, and the righteousness of Christ was the goal in the lives of our children – a key component of Christian character.

I asked for joy for our journey into the education of the principles and the living out of them as we prepared our children to take back the liberties that the enemy has stolen, in their faith in Christ, in the power of His Word and the FIRE of His Holy Spirit.

Here are the scriptures He gave me to encourage me:

> *"You will show me the path of life; In Your presence is fullness of joy; At Your right hand are pleasures forevermore"* ***(Psalms 16:11 NKJV)***.

> *"It is a joy for the just to do justice, but destruction will come to the workers of iniquity"* ***(Proverbs 21:15 NKJV)***.

> *"For you shall go out with joy, and be led out with peace; The mountains and the hills Shall break forth into singing before you, and all the trees of the field shall clap their hands"* ***(Isaiah 55:12 NKJV)***.

The Lord gave me ***Isaiah 55*** in the 1980's. Joy is a big part of my relationship with Him.

Last night He gave me ***James 1:2-4***: *"My brethren, count it all joy when you fall into various trials, knowing that the testing of your faith produces patience. But let patience have its perfect work, that you may be perfect and complete, lacking nothing."*

C.S. Lewis captured it in his Narnia Chronicles, The Lion, the Witch and the Wardrobe. After Aslan was executed by the witch, Lucy and Susan were crying and as the dawn arrived the stone table cracked in two, and suddenly Aslan stood before them bigger than ever.

Then the most amazing thing happened. The very thing that I know is missing in the teaching of the Principles. Aslan began to "romp" around the girls – up and down the hill, back and forth until the girls and the lion ran into each other and rolled down the hill in a heap, laughing.

Do you see it? JOY. And the book of Hebrews says in Chapter 1 that because Jesus loved righteousness and hated lawlessness, He was given more joy than His companions.

Aslan reflected that joy even in the hard, sad times. He is our example. So how do I communicate something that will be hard to accept, something that will seem "Preposterous" and overwhelming to get a handle on for small children?

If children learn that discipline and patience are times of growth and opportunities to find joy, Christian character will form and the fruit of that is virtue, initiative, industry, diligence and, hard-work.

The Oxford dictionary defines industry in governmental terms – *"an industrious people striving to make their country prosperous."*

Parents, start early to develop Christian Character in your children. When little children begin to hear you say over and over how precious they are and they have talents and abilities to discover there is a confidence and a peace in their daily activities.

Children have such innocence until they don't. What they learn to believe about themselves affects how they see the world around them. Discovering their individuality reveals the diversity of God's creation.

When self-government and individuality reflect God's ruling in the heart of the child it will lead to an ability to recognize and rule in their lives when they become adults.

And when God is ruling in the heart, self-government and individuality, in concert with the hard decisions and actions of life, form Christian Character.

Nathan is now a grown man. I recently asked him if he thought the Principle Approach to education benefitted him and prepared him for adulthood. Here is his response:

> *It's one thing to read history and study literature from the lens of classic humanist development. But it's entirely another to study history from the context of an overarching Divine Plan. While I was young when it was taught, something I distinctly remember from the Principle Approach is how it went beyond discussing just the granular causal reasons for historical*

events and what we can learn about it. Instead it attempted a Herculean feat, which is to also lay out the guiding hand of the Divine across history. When you're young, this not only helps ground your belief in the goodness of God despite (and in the midst of) man's terrible history, but it gives a foundational understanding of how to think about things when they happen in your own life. If God's hand can be seen across the triumphs and suffering of history then it can surely be seen across the triumphs and suffering of your own life. And the awe-inspired fear of a Divine Hand is the beginning of wisdom.

Chapter 5 – The Christian Idea of the Child

I want to define the terms I mentioned earlier.

Government - The flow or activity of power and force; direction, regulation, control, restraint. Who or what is in control.

Providence - God; God's immediate care and supervision of His creation. Working through men and events to advance His liberty and law.

Individuality - Everything in Gods universe is revelational of Gods infinity, God's diversity, God's individuality. God creates distinct individuals. God maintains the identity and individuality of everything he created.

Conscience - The principle or faculty within which decisions are made upon the lawfulness or unlawfulness of our own actions and affections and instantly condemns or approves them

Principle - The cause, source, or origin of anything. Principles are foundational to our thinking, our world view, and our understanding. Principles cause an effect that is visible and external, but reflecting the internal.

The vision that was presented for my children when being taught by the Principle Approach was so desirable. It is reflective learning, thoughtfully done with careful research, reasoning, relating and recording (not just fill in the blank or multiple choice). The primary grades are the soil-softening and germinating years for the good fruit to come. All seeds and good seeds are planted by God and watered by His word, but some won't bear fruit until later in life. The early grades bring the forming of good habits, the beginning of work skills, the attitudes, the interests, and the strategies of learning, but all form the basis of scholarship.

Viewing my children through the Christian idea of the Child means affirming their wholeness and imparting a sense of their particular, individual purpose in God's providence.

My job as their mother and teacher was to nurture and cultivate whatever resided in each heart by the gift of God through inspiration, consecration and instruction. Let me just say this was a level of personal discipline I had never been called on to experience or cultivate for my own life.

There was a poem I taught the kids:

STARTING WITH ME.
God made me special like no one else you see,
God made me a witness to His diversity.
~ Rosalie June Slater

There is so much more to the learning of this curriculum. It is transformative, requiring great measures of my time to prepare and understand. It required major focus, and I was in the time of my life when I could give 100% to it and to my children.

Many moms today start their family while they are young and need to be a contributor to the financial standing of their homes. One income is not enough and if it is a single parent home then one income is all they have.

So, I guess the question becomes - How could a parent, particularly a single parent, prepare themselves to teach their children the Principles of American Christian Education? It is more needed now than when I taught it to my children.

This is how God led me and I am sure He will lead every parent who wants to secure the liberty of Christ in their children's' heart. Each child, and each parent, is led individually by The Lord with Holy Spirit FIRE. He does not put it on you; you must desire it. I pray you will desire His FIRE.

Chapter 6 - The Fruit of Our Labors of Love

Grandchildren, another generation given as a blessing from the Lord. Each one unique and special in their own way.

Since my husband and I do not have everyday access to our grandchildren we approach informing and impacting their life experience with picture books filled with more information about their identity in Christ and the liberty He brings when He rules in their heart from a young age. We gained this information from our experience with our own children.

Levi was our first. He had some difficulty, but came through it and continues to progress. As always, he is fearfully and wonderfully made.

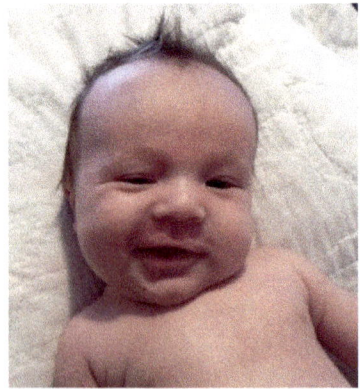 

There he is. New beginnings for him and for Mary and Brandon.

The new mommy and daddy with Levi William Emerson, he is already the light of the world. Do you believe that babies come by the will of God or only by the will of the flesh? I believe a baby comes from a far greater plan than the pleasure or violence of the joining of two or all the many scientific ways babies can be born.

There is a greater plan and that plan begins and ends with God.

Many of the things I write can be found in the Holy Scriptures, yet we, who value the WORD of God don't know the fullness of His WORD. As I continue to experience life with our grandchildren it becomes more real that there is a greater plan that we are a part of, and babies are able to know the plan as a seed planted by God begins to unfold in their lives.

We are privileged to help in the discovery of what is planted by God in each life. No two are the same. Each one is individually made by God and given to us to steward.

May I just say, knowing God was going to steer my parenting on the best course was a relief. So now I have to believe He will steer my daughter and her husband on the best course for their children, and my son and his wife; and if either veer from the course, HE will help get them back on course.

You see, every child is the hope of their generation. Every child is given by God providentially for their generation.

Next, we welcomed Lennon Russell Emerson in his family's life and his world.

 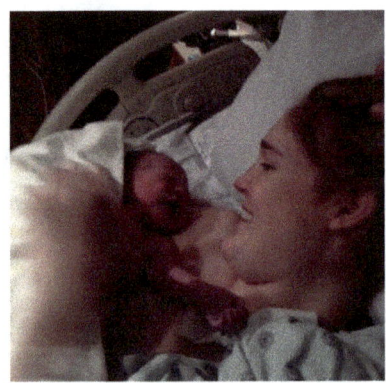

Then a little sister was born into the family. Levi asked his mommy for a little sister and he got one. Do you think God heard his asking as a prayer and answered? Yes, it was an "asking" from his little heart, and it is our heart that communicates with our Creator, and language is the vehicle. Not the only vehicle – some things are better communicated without words, and that is our ability to communicate through the gate of wisdom in the power of Holy Spirit and the FIRE, once ignited, that burns within each one.

Here's the sister Levi asked for, Livian Derby Emerson. Now they are a family of five, plus cats and dogs.

As I was saying about Levi asking his mommy for a sister. He used not only a language of words for her, but a language of the heart, heard by God.

Words are given as a gift for communicating with one another and with God. Words are powerful. They are like the rudder of a ship. They can steer us in any direction.

Livi is now turning three. Recently when we had the grandkids for the day, I incorporated some elements of a Bible story into our activities. I told them how much Jesus loves them (identity in Christ), and that He will help them be kind, share, ask with "Please and thank you," and use words to communicate instead of hitting or whining. Sometimes I tell them self-government is when they are careful about the amount of sugar they eat, and when they put their toys away.

There is a book about sweet rhyming prayers Children have prayed to God, and I read it to Livi for the first time yesterday. Her brothers were away feeding the neighbor's fish with Pawpaw, so it was just me, Livi and JESUS. As I read, I used a lot of vocal elocution and joy just to make the prayers even more exciting. Every time I would say, "look at me, God, or Can You see me God, or Look, God, or Watch me God," she would give me the sweetest smile.

I think she understood what the children were saying and to whom.

Here is a picture of the book.

Every language is given to communicate with one another and with God. Some people groups communicate with one another but have not learned how to communicate with their Creator. That's why Jesus said to go and make disciples of every nation, baptizing them in the name of the Father, Son and Holy Spirit, and that He would be with them.

Once the language of relationship with God Is known, the assurance of His presence always becomes known. Just think, communicating with the Father of all and He knows your language and your name.

Lennon knows Jesus is in His heart. I asked him one day if he knew Jesus and he said, "Yes, and He's in my heart.

So here is one more "preposterous" truth: God knows each and every name of our children, because they were, and are, His. I'll let you think about the verbs in this statement, past and present – but let's not stop there – and future. Now that is "preposterous."

I'm going to get ahead of myself just a little here to say that even the names of my grandchildren's children are known by God.

"PREPOSTEROUS!" You say. Not really. Everything is finished in God's eternity. So He sees the entire beginning and end of linear time because His time is eternal. And He has assured a wonderful beginning and ending of time by placing it all in HIS Son. And when we come to Him, we return to the eternal time of our creation. And all things are consummated in Christ, in whom we have the assurance of God's best in each one.

Every generation is seen by God in their providential place.

Ok, here is another grandchild. Our son, Nathan and his wife, Emily have a daughter, Lily Rose Mapp. We don't see each other as often, but the older she gets the more we FaceTime together.

As I'm writing this book she just called and wanted Me and Pawpaw to come to her party with her Minnie's and Sky, from "Paw Patrol." We brought our Minnie and Rubble from "Paw Patrol" to clear the way to the party. Through FaceTime we played for a while, but then she wanted to watch a TV show so we said good bye and sent our love. This is our Lily with her mom and dad.

On John's birthday Lily called to tell her Pawpaw that Jesus loves him. She's just three years old. What a gift for Pawpaw.

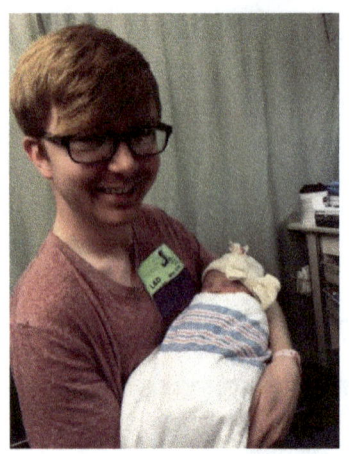

There she is with her mommy and daddy. A gift from God to her family and her world. I don't know about you, but thinking beyond the family is not even in your mind when you are a new mommy or daddy, but the truth is, inside these precious babes is planted an entire long life of promise and possibility, by God.

And like I said before, God's word is the best Manual of instructions for parenting. It is the best there is.

We have our 5th grandchild on the way. He will be born in March 2022. His name is Elliot Allen Mapp. It is my hope to be permitted by his parents to pray Holy Spirit FIRE over him with the laying on of hands.

These precious grandchildren are living in a different time. The children's shows like "Daniel Tiger" aren't readily available. Many of the cartoon characters are not even close to being real, and the message they bring is not often about kindness and goodness. To help them remember who they are and who God is, I have prepared four Shutterfly books with pictures and text for them to look at when they are older. An example is prepared for you in Appendix 1.

In their home, the story of who they are in Christ continues. And honestly, if we could know their thoughts, Jesus is always talking with them, telling them how precious they are to Him. As I was editing this book for publication, I had an opportunity to share the

Children's Prayer Book with Livi, our granddaughter, once again. Her other grandmother had just been hospitalized so I asked her if she wanted to pray for Grandma.

We prayed and she then said something very interesting. I don't know if it is prophecy, but she said things she couldn't have naturally known. She said her grandma was happy with God and she could breathe. Livi is three and has heard her parents talking about her grandma's condition, which is very serious, but I can't believe she has the mental capacity to know about her breathing, or that God would be with her. So, for me, this is an example of Jesus talking with her.

The following is an introduction which I included in Levi's book, and his Pawpaw included a special word for him as well.

Pawpaw's introduction applies not only our children, but all of Gods children.

Why Expose Babies to the Deep Principles of God? John A. Mapp, Jr.

> *In the last few years, neuroscientists have come to understand that individual thoughts are not contained within single brain cells, or collections of cells, but imprinted throughout the cerebral cortex, much like the image in a hologram that is recorded in every part of the holographic material. Short term thoughts and memories are recorded in brain waves; long term thoughts and memories are recorded across brain structures that are subtly shaped by brain waves over time. Thus, thoughts and memories are pure information stored by the brain. Thoughts and memories are therefore mass-less, and have wave properties rather than physical dimensions. This, in turn, means that they take on the Quantum Mechanical attribute of non-locality. Our very consciousness, therefore, must be non-material and non-local, meaning that our consciousness, or soul, if you will, is not confined to the spatial or temporal boundaries of our physical lives on the earth.*

C. S. Lewis pointed out that a man is not a body that has a soul; he is a soul that has a body. He understood that our consciousness, our very essence, exists beyond this earthly realm. By exposing infants to the Word of God and the principles of God's Kingdom, we are edifying their souls, their inner beings, at a spiritual level that transcends the physical.

As parents and grandparents, we also have God-given authority over our children and grandchildren. Jesus understood authority, and commended others who likewise understood it. The act of proclaiming God's blessings and principles over our babies gives the Lord, who is Sovereign, but ever the gentleman, free reign to work in the lives of these little ones and order their steps and their development according to His highest and best plan for their lives.

My Introduction to Baby Books follows:

I am a 65-year-old first time grandmother. I have known the humor of God first hand. Married at 38, first child at 40 and second child at 42. Now I'm a grandmother. From child birth to the present my journey of faith required great change. The change I am referring to is how we instruct our children for life and when we begin that instruction.

I am sure there are many books on child rearing, but interestingly enough there were no baby books on how to introduce the baby to the truths of faith in the Living God. According to "the experts," babies are too young to grasp that they need a Savior and that Jesus is the Savior that reveals their identity in Christ. And we can't force a young child to confess Christ and their need of a Savior. They wouldn't understand what they were saying, even if they could talk.

I regret that I listened to "the experts." I was extremely insecure as a new mom at 40 and believed they knew more than I did about my baby. That was a big mistake; please don't make the same mistake I have made.

Now as my children are grown and have children of their own, I am able with more confidence in God and His Word to believe we have missed something in our child rearing. He has given Holy Spirit to reveal even to the unspeaking infants a wisdom greater than the wisdom of the world, as written in the gospel of Luke

I now have first-hand information from other parents who have heard amazing things from their children who said God told them something and it came true. They range in age from one to four years old.

We have underestimated what babies are capable of knowing about God, and that they can even Know God.

I believe babies can know their identity in Christ at a very young age, possibly even before they can talk. It has happened before. We see accounts of things happening before their time; for example – The future was brought into the present time when David went into the Holy of Holies and got the show bread because his men were hungry. The wedding at Cana when Jesus filled the jars with wine, even while saying it was not yet his time, or when young Samuel heard the Lord calling him, when The Lord had been silent for 400 years.

So, I say we can awaken in our children at a young age, what God has already put in them.

Jesus knew. He said, *"Let the children come to me...of such is the kingdom of God."*

This about sums up beautifully what I/we believe about teaching our babies that God knows them and has an awesome plan for their lives hidden for them to discover. They, with the help of parents, guardians, teacher, and others figure out what their part is in their world and act, in the FIRE power of God within them. Yahoo!

Chapter 7 - Jenna with 2 n's

Jenna is one of the young moms that is awakening in her children their identity in Christ and their relationship with Holy Spirit. I have invited her to share about her experiences and her children's experiences.

When Jenna was in high school, our church offered a program for the youth. Any adult who felt led could select one of the youths to mentor and disciple. I chose Jenna.

I didn't really know Jenna, I only observed her from afar as a powerful worship dancer. My first meaningful experience with her was to bring a bouquet to her school for her. She was a senior and graduation was just around the corner.

She still tells the story of the life changing importance one kind act was to her. I was unaware but God knew and He put it into my heart to bring her flowers.

Little did I know, in all her years as a fabulous dancer and as the lead in many of her school plays, Jenna had never received flowered from her parents. They just weren't aware of the way to say, "hey you are great, you danced or performed so amazingly," by giving a bouquet at the end of the performance.
Jenna said she understood, but when she received the bouquet I

brought, she knew it was from the Lord and it meant so much more to her.

We continued to keep in touch and became very dear to each other. We encouraged each other in our faith walk. I don't think she thought she helped me, but she did, and still, I am always learning from her encounters with The Lord.

Jenna married Troy Sartor and then she and Troy had two amazing boys. Along with the responsibility of children, she was called by God to counsel women and teach Bible studies. Her Amazing relationship with the Lord is flowing in her life with her family and the women that she has befriended along life's path.

I communicated with her regarding the education of her boys, and recently my husband and I were able to visit. The following will be conversations we had about the boys' relationship with the Lord and the events in their lives. But first I would like to share a story.

Jenna's youngest son RJ connected with me when he had just arrived home from the hospital. It was one of those spiritual connections, and I was curious what it might mean. I now know that the connection was a connection of the FIRE power, dunamis, of Holy Spirit. The Lord reminded me of the Gospel stories when He felt virtue leave Him when He ministered to the people. The word for virtue is dunamis, and dunamis is power from on high, resident in Jesus, the Son of God by the power of Holy Spirit. I felt His virtue, resident in me, leave. I was holding RJ so he received from The Lord that day dunamis power, which I call FIRE power. OR, I received power from RJ. Either way FIRE was transferred.

I wondered what our connection would be after a few years. Also, her oldest son Brendon was always the happiest and most sensitive little boy. He was always full of smiles and stories to share. In their new home in Tennessee, he is a little more reserved, but his smile is just as big and his intuitive abilities are beyond his years.

RJ is a very passionate and warm, with a fiery personality.
Our conversation begins:

Jenna: A little boy kept taking RJ's BeyBlade toys even after RJ asked him to stop. RJ took the toy into another area, but the boy followed and continued to bother RJ. Finally, RJ hauled off and hit him. Troy and I teach the boys about the need to resolve a disagreement peacefully, but RJ said he could not.

Jenna: The little boy told his mother and then she came to talk to me. I told her I would speak to RJ. I talked with him about forgiveness. RJ is not one to say he's sorry and he held his anger toward that little boy for a week.

Jenna: So after a week RJ decided to ask Jesus to forgive him. This is his first time asking for forgiveness. We were driving to one of our co-ops in Florida and a skywriter wrote "Jesus Forgives" in the sky.

Jenna: Look RJ look, Jesus wrote it in the sky for you. (Laughter.) It was just amazing that that was sooo clear. "You are forgiven." It took him six days to forgive, and Jesus made it abundantly clear for RJ that he was forgiven.

The Brendon encounter:

Jenna: Brendon had gotten onto a website that I wasn't prepared for him to see. I started freaking out. I started coming up with a plan, "check all technology, everything, smash it with hammers. Satan, you are not coming to get my child."

Jenna: And so, on the Monday night Unending Progress Zoom Call I taught about control. We did an activation. We opened our hands to release whatever we were holding onto. When we opened our hands I asked, "Lord, what am I holding on to? I hold my hands up to you and surrender whatever is in my hand and trust you to be in control."

Jenna: He showed me the technology and Brendon. And so, we asked, "what's true?" Then the Lord said, "Brendon is full of integrity, he has self-control, he comes to you when something's not right, he doesn't repeat something he's not supposed to. He's going to receive this like punishment as if he's been bad, but you can trust him."

Jenna: "OK," and then He showed me that's what my parents did to me. They treated me like I was bad when I wasn't. It was hard for me to connect with them because if I said anything I'd be in trouble. My intention wasn't to be disrespectful. I asked questions because I didn't understand."

Jenna: So I went to Brendon, I was crying, and I said, "Sweety, this is what the Lord says about you. He says you are full of integrity. Do you know what that means?" He said, "No." "That means you're doing the right thing when no one is watching. God sees that. He says that you are trustworthy and the Holy Spirit has given you self-control so mommy doesn't have to control you."

Jenna: Brendon said "I do those things, I do." I said, "it was so scary for Mommy and I want to protect you. And so it makes me want to control you but I believe what God says about you is true.

John: Do you know what that imparts to Brendon? It imparts a sense of agency, that he is responsible, that he can make choices.

Jenna: yes, yes.

John: He can make responsible choices. I don't mean "agency" in the sense of, "the captain of his ship, and the master of his fate," but he has the freedom to make responsible choices for himself, and not listen to others who would lead him into temptation or make wrong choices for him, exerting inappropriate control over him, or, as he grows, take away his rights as a citizen.

Kathy: He'll recognize the wrong control and say no. Either verbally, or in his head. And then he'll reason, what's the right response.

John: Before we came, we had dinner with JoAnn, the woman you prayed for during COVID and her son, Scott. He told Kathy what she was talking about was called "agency."

Kathy: I said I was writing a book. And I was describing what I taught at a child's level, which was self-government, individuality, conscience being the most sacred of properties, and Christian character. I was describing how important it is for children to know these things while they are young, so that when they get older, it will be like riding a bike. It will pop up in their head when someone is trying to control them and it's not their right. And so, the child will know, and they can say, "Hey, no, I'm not doing that."

Kathy: What you're teaching your son is that in his heart is the sovereign rule of Christ Jesus that gives him the wisdom to say to you what he said and respond with agency. That's the point.

Jenna: the next day he said "Mommy you could be doing 10-15 second shorts about Jesus, while doing dishes - How Jesus washes every sin away. Or treating a stain in the laundry - how Jesus gets out every stain of sin, but mommy it has to be only 15 seconds. No one is going to listen to 20 minutes.

Jenna: So Brendon said, "you try one and I'll be finished before you finish writing. So he did do some and he called them, Mommy, Jesus and her Son. Look at the liberty he had to use technology for good creatively. He was motivated, not burdened with unnecessary control.

Another event:

Jenna: Brendon's friend was having a birthday party and the theme was Harry Potter. Brendon didn't want to go, and I asked him why. He said, "That's witchcraft and I don't want to come." I didn't really know what Harry Potter was. I had never heard of it, and having no interest in knowing about it, I didn't know it was witchcraft.

Jenna: Brendon told his friend he didn't want to watch a Harry Potter movie and his friend said, "If you're coming to my party, you'll have to watch the movie." And Brendon said, "Well, then, I'm not coming to your party."

Jenna: His friend changed his entire party theme to Parrot Mountain, because he wanted Brendon to come to his party.

Kathy: Wow, That's the most beautiful example of Conscience being Brendon's most sacred property. His conscience wouldn't let him go.

Kids need to know they can tell their friends 'no' if it goes against their conscience.

Jenna: And I thought how powerful for Brendon to see, "I'm going to be who I really am and I am still loved." I don't often have that happen for myself, but how powerful. I've never given him any opinion about anything to do with witchcraft.

Kathy: Cool. He who rules in his heart has given it to him.

Jenna: I remember he never liked the Disney films. He hated them. It was the evil. He couldn't stand the evil so we never watched them. We watched "Cars," with Mater and McQueen. You know, that's what he likes. There's no evil, no Ursula, no Jafar. So recently someone gave us their subscription to Disney Plus. We tried to watch a movie: "Here's one, 'Brave,' let's watch this." Like 10 minutes in the girl goes to a sorcerer to have a spell cast. He said, "I feel sick. I can't watch this." So, we didn't.

Jenna went on to tell about other encounters Brandon had with an atmosphere of unbelief or evil. He is extremely sensitive to both. One of Jenna's family members says she's a Christian but doesn't really live the life of a Christian. Brendon was left in her care once and when Jenna came for him, he said he didn't ever want to be with his cousin without Jenna. Jenna agreed, knowing his sensitivity to the atmosphere around him.

Additional comments from RJ and Brendon:

This was also shared during our visit to the Sartor home in August.

Brendan sees the flood as the kindness of God, purifying the whole earth forever. And God was so kind to rescue Jonah from the whale even though Jonah was running from Him.

When Jenna asked RJ what God had given him to share with the earth, he took his hands and went around his face and said, "This majestical face."

This is a recommended reading by Jenna, for Christian parents who want to understand the philosophies being taught to children of all ages that draw the children away from their Christian upbringing. It points out the pitfalls in Marxist foundational thinking. Chapter 17 will discuss that in more detail.

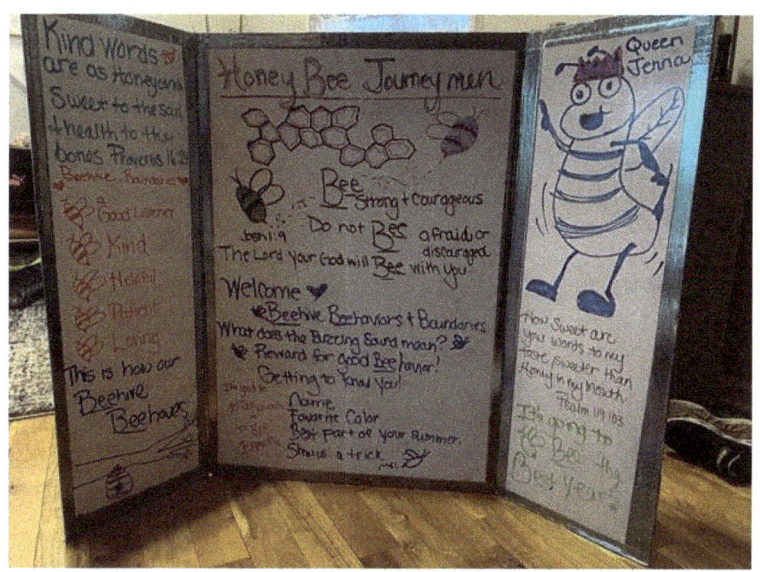

This is Jenna's Home School Orientation Board. This board represents government at the classroom level. Her orientation board represents for each child the rules of the classroom and the agency in which they were drafted (Bible is the order to be followed). It is a classroom constitution. It is for kindness, recognition, respect and safety of all who agree with it; but without the voluntary agreement of each one the classroom could become chaos. The understanding received in this classroom ripples out into the family, which has rules that must be followed according to the Word of God. Or, it is already being modeled in the home, so it's possible to be followed in the classroom. So the classroom and the home are a child's first experience with self-government, which leads to agency in their life. **Agency means - moving and exerting power, action: as the agency of Providence in the natural world.**

I found myself thinking back to our orientations when my children were the age of hers. As I looked at her Orientation Board, I remembered we would introduce the importance of establishing order through written documents like a "classroom constitution" and Classroom rules of conduct, which she illustrates on her orientation board.

As Jenna is led by the Holy Spirit into the best teaching philosophy for her children, so was I, and so is every mom who wants to help their child discover who they are in Christ. Their true identity is hidden in Christ and is revealed step by step. And I now believe it is Holy Spirit FIRE that burns away whatever might be hindering or hiding their identity.

Jenna posted recently a beautiful summary of her care for her children:

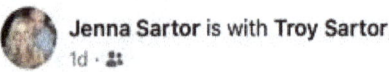

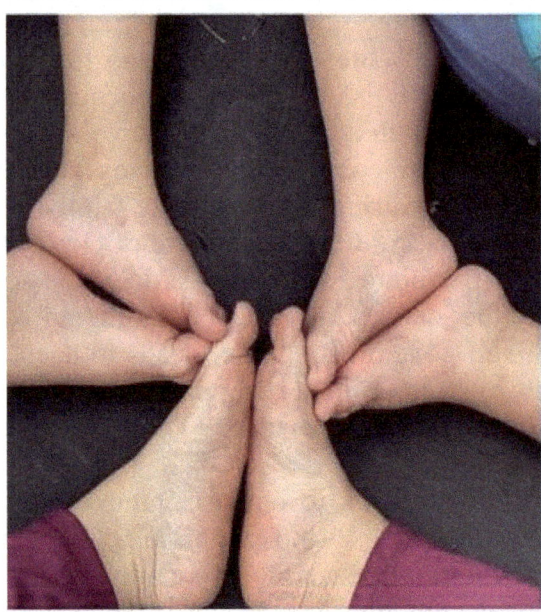

💪 I'm wholly aware that alone this would be utterly impossible. But I'm not alone, I'm in Christ!

👼 He is with me, and He loves these beautiful feet more than I do!

🌍 He knows the plans He has for them!
As I seek Him, He can teach me, moment by moment, on how to lead them into truth- that will keep them free!

🤴 I find great hope for their future knowing that I don't have to know, I just look up consistently asking Jesus for help, and begin to understand that is exactly what I need to model to them to do so they can have all things added unto them!

📖 Proverbs 22:6
6 Train up a child in the way he should go: and when he is old, he will not depart from it.

📖 John 14:20
On that day you will realize that I am in my Father, and you are in me, and I am in you.

📖 Jeremiah 29:11
11 For I know the plans I have for you," declares the LORD, "plans to prosper you and not to harm you, plans to give you hope and a future.

📖 John 16:13
But when he, the Spirit of truth, comes, he will guide you into all the truth. He will not speak on his own; he will speak only what he hears, and he will tell you what is yet to come.

📖 Matthew 7:7
"Ask and it will be given to you; seek and you will find; knock and the door will be opened to you.

📖 Matthew 6:33
Seek the Kingdom of God above all else, and live righteously, and he will give you everything you need.

Chapter 8 - Children Who Can Fly

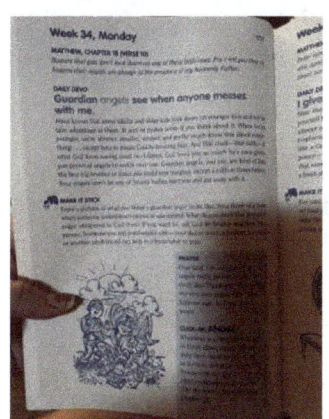

These drawings were created by Brendon and RJ Sartor in response to their morning meditations facilitated by their mother. The very big, bold, and powerful painting is by RJ. He calls it "Worship" – it's his expression of worship. And it was "Morning meditation on the goodness and love of God and seeing His angels deliver gifts and minister to us."

Some of the home school moms with Jenna sent me some of their children's encounters with God.
Sent to me on 8/9 from Jenna Sartor about children she knows in her home school group:

Wyatt Man – The most impactful to me – age 5. When playing his Kindle, he felt God tell him that it was becoming an idol in his life. He put it on the shelf and hasn't picked it up since because he doesn't want anything to become an idol in his life.

Phone message – "When Peyton was 3, she heard music coming from down by the lake at (Jenna's) your house and she turned to me and said,'Jesus is down there.' Then when Sadie was around 3, she told us Jesus was with her and He ate her sandwich."

Alexia – "When she was four she began learning about the human body, health and safety. She felt urged to pray for Grammy's sister, whom she had never met, nor even knew about, because she was going to die from black lungs. We found out a few days later Aunt Peggy had lung cancer. She did pass away two years later after a failed treatment."

This is from Amelia's mom – "I learned something from my four-years-old daughter recently. We were talking about Jesus, and she told me He died on the cross for our sins. Wanting to gauge her understanding I asked, 'What is sin?' She said, 'Sin is when we think we are stronger than God.' Mind Blown!!!!! Her four –year-old theology just defined mine a bit more clearly…."

Here are some photos and paintings of my grandchildren and the character they demonstrate at their young age:

Lennon – "The Gymnast"

Livi – "Fearless"

Levi – "The Sillies"

Lennon – "A Happy Boy"

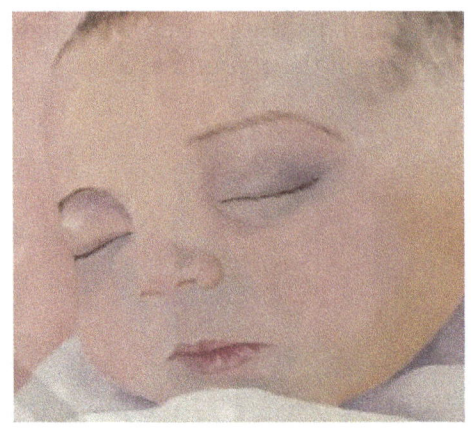

Lily – "Peace"

and "Joy"

Lennon –
"Oh, the Wonder and the joy"

Livi – "Happy Discovery"

Mary – "The Singer"

The wonderful ways of children- They see the world through a very different lens. We were tagged in this post from a friend in Florida.

Chapter 9 – Jenna's Unending Progress

Jenna's topic for this session was "Rest, Trust, and Worship" - the three factors that are key to allowing God to remain in control. They are also key to embracing the FIRE when we find ourselves in it. We don't have to be afraid when we know the consuming FIRE, Himself, is already in us and we are in Him.

"Tonight, let's begin to deepen our understanding of the purpose and power of the FIRE of God."

I was invited to participate. Most of those that joined the session were known by each other – Family and Sisters in the faith.

Jenna had some amazing insight into the FIRE of God. New revelation. The kind of revelation that requires a seeking heart and a large dose of Holy Spirit alive and active.

Prayer followed the teaching. Beautiful, powerful, breakthrough prayer. One of the ladies had to leave the session early so we prayed for her and her family. Then her twin sister brought her concern for prayer.

This was a wonderful example of conscience being a sacred property that God protects valiantly. Her daughter has a situation at school that violates her conscience. Her roommates smoke weed in the apartment when she's at work. Everything in the apartment smells of weed and beer bottles, and other messes are in the apartment nightly.

She called her mom but hesitated to tell her everything. As the largeness of the problem surfaced through conversation, her mom's "mother bear" rose up and she was ready to act.

Her daughter didn't want to stir things up. She didn't want to be a tattle tale. As I listened, I heard an important life principle in action and shared my thought.

Kathy: "It's an important matter of conscience. I said to the mom that her daughter's conscience is troubled by all the behaviors of her roommates. She doesn't even want to go home. I believe with all my heart, that if she has the courage to speak up it will be not only her voice, but a greater authority will be heard, and hearts and minds could change for good." The greater authority I was speaking of was the authority of God heard in her words. Mom wasn't convinced, because there were illegal drugs involved and her daughter was under age for drinking. She felt the need to go to the school and talk to the school authority."

Gretchen: "After hearing the explanation of conscience being the most sacred property that God has given my friends daughter, she had a vision of a scene in the Lion King where Simba had gone into the 'Bad Lands' and the hyenas were harassing him. Simba said he wasn't afraid of them and roared, his tiny roar. Of course, they laughed. He wasn't affected by their mocking and roared again. This time the sound was mighty and terrifying. Simba's father had arrived and roared with Simba. The hyenas knew that sound and ran. Simba never doubted he was the child of the King. And when Mufasa showed up he had his Father's authority."

What a confirming word from a child's cartoon. And here's a photographer's caption:

So I believe, just as Brendon spoke his conscience regarding the theme of a party and the boy having the party changed the party theme so Brendon would come, her daughter could speak with the same authority and things would change. And the change would be for the better because of the authority that is greater backing her up – standing behind her.

Another thing I am thinking as I hear more and more stories of conscience leading to change in the hearts and minds of children and from children to adults: This generation has been equipped with a clear conscience, and when salvation is needed it comes. One of the things Jesus does is purge the conscience from dead works when new life in Him is provided.

A little child shall lead them – and of such is the Kingdom of God. This is what Jesus meant when He spoke to the disciples to let the children come to him.

This world needs changing and our children are equipped to be the change agents. They have agency – the quality of moving or exerting power as the agency of Providence in the natural world. And they have Holy Spirit FIRE power. That FIRE can make you brave.

I'm going to encourage you to watch Jenna's video – "Brave Part 1" at:

https://m.youtube.com/watch?v=-O7QEp4eEXE&feature=youtu.be

Chapter 10 – Gretchen

I asked Gretchen about her children's personal relationship with Jesus. When did she become aware of their ability to communicate with Him?

Gretchen: Annabelle just has an understanding. She wasn't taught. It's just there.

Kathy: Is there anything in particular you might be able to remember Annabelle saying when she was little that is an example of what you just summed up?

Gretchen: One of the things that blew me away was when she was four. She was in the back seat of the car, and I was talking about a dog that I wanted and she said, "Mommy, you'll have to choose." And I said, "What do you mean?" She said, "You'll have to choose between a dog and a baby."

And I said, "Well, then I want the baby." Because that was back when we were wanting another baby. And I said it mockingly like, "Well, when is that going to happen?" And I threw my hands in the air, because we had been trying for four years.

She said, "The baby will come into your belly in 90 days and you will have your baby in August." I was like, "What!" And began to laugh and then I really laughed because it played out mathematically from when she said it until 9 months for the baby to come."

"It just came out of her mouth. She had no idea what she was saying. So I said, 'Annabelle, did God tell you that?' Because there was no other explanation and she said, 'Yep. He told me in my ear.'"

"So, to this day it has never happened, however all of the stuff God has brought up lately, while in Kansas City and in August, I asked, 'Am I hearing You correctly?' He would confirm. And so, I know it's going to happen soon because He told me to start taking folic acid. So, we'll see if it's this year. I think what she did was prophecy. She doesn't know math nor the gestation period for babies to be born."

Kathy: "You know what I think is cool? She was seeing from the eternal perspective which is always 'NOW.'"

Gretchen: "She told everyone, 'My mommy is going to have a baby.' And my friends would ask me if I was pregnant, and I would say, 'No,' but she said I was."

Gretchen: "Here's another one. When Annabelle was seven and she had a dream, it was during the time we were fostering and we had Noah, and we had decided we needed to move so we would have more room. We were eating one day and Annabelle left the table and came over to us and said, 'God just told me, I'm going to allow you to move, because of your reasoning why you're moving, but I'm going to give you what you need, not what you want.'"

"Then she described what she saw. She saw builders building a home; well, the way she described it we knew it was a home because it was a square with bricks going up. So when we found a home we knew we were supposed to get they were building around the corner exactly what she had seen. And the home we found was what she said. It was the house we needed, but it was not the house I liked. I liked that house the least of any house we had ever had. But, yep, it was the house we needed. It had the big basement we could use for fostering Noah and the teenager we temporarily had; and after the teenager left, my Aunt Sue lived in it temporarily until she found a home."

Chapter 11 - Nations That Know You Not Will Come to You. Nelly, Maria, Lupe, Dr. Nicku Kungu Mordi

This chapter is about the women and families the Lord has sent to me, and vice versa. While living in Florida I began a 501(c)(3) tax exempt corporation as a ministry to Mexican children and families.

Nelly -

The Catholic Social Services sent a woman to me who is still an important part of my life; Nelly and her entire family are like family to my husband and me. When she came to me, she had just escaped from an abusive husband. He had beaten her, and her oldest daughter and a neighbor helped her get away.

I can't remember all the details from the beginning, but I began to assist with material things and immigration process expenses.

As she trusted me to help her, she shared her story and we also began the legal process to get a restraining order against the girls' father because he had returned to Florida and was driving by their house.

We compiled all the paperwork and paid all the fees and the court date was set. We arrived and went to the area where her hearing was to be, and she saw the girls' father coming into the room. They were called into the court room and they returned very quickly.
It seems the Florida laws see parents as jointly responsible and able to

care for children independently of the other. The judge rejected my friend's request and told the father to go to the fourth floor to apply for joint custody – not the outcome we had hoped for.

Shortly after that he appeared at her home and asked to see the girls. There was not a legal right he had acquired; it was just a father's request. He said he had changed, and she allowed him to visit in the yard with the girls. They enjoyed the visit and he came on the weekend to visit three or four times in the following months.

One day he asked to take them to McDonalds. This would be the first time they would be alone with their father away from their home, but he had gained my friend's trust. She wanted to believe he had changed.

Unfortunately, he kidnapped the girls. He had them for three weeks, and there was nothing my friend could do to get them back. The police could not go to the house where they were because the judge had ruled against her restraining order against the father of the girls. No police officer in any Florida county could go to the home where he had them because of the judge's ruling.

This is the most amazing example of the government that God did not intend our nation to have. Civil government was to have NO jurisdiction in personal family matters. Yet, in this case, they did. But the judge's ruling did not solve this family's problem. It was resolved by the family members themselves in a more final way than a judge's ruling forcing him to stay away from them ever could have.

Recall the Bible story of the woman who kept knocking on her neighbor's door for bread, and finally he rose up and gave it to her. Her persistence drove him to comply with her request. It was the same in this situation.

The Father of the girls took their phones away from them so they couldn't call their mother, and after three weeks they cried and cried and cried and cried until he couldn't take it anymore and returned the girls to their mother.
They, the children, decided they did not ever want to see their dad

again. He tricked them, he lied to them, and he lied to their mother. They told him they didn't want to see him ever again and to this day he has not returned.

Actually, I believe he was deported back to Mexico, because it was determined that the woman he was living with was not his wife, and he had filed papers stating that she was his wife, but she was married to another man. Falsifying government documents is a felony punishable by deportation.

Here is a beautiful example of how government was not the answer in this family's life. My friend and I and others prayed during this entire debacle. I was mad at God, but she trusted Him to help her. She had been delivered from many dangers throughout her life and she Trusted HIM.

He did what He said He would do. Government was not the answer.

She continues to experience the failure of law and government to work on her behalf to get her immigration papers before a judge for residency. But it doesn't matter. Her character is known by teachers, doctors, employers, the elderly, her neighbors, and me. She has a green card that is renewable, and she can work, drive, and care for her six children. She has even married a fine man that the children love. Her character opens doors for her all the time. She is a child of God and her children are learning to be, as she leads them by example.

Maria -

Maria and her brothers and sisters were the first Mexican children I met, while helping with an after-school program in Center Hill, FL. There were many children in the program, but her family was, and is still, a part of my husband's and my life.

Soon it wasn't just the children, but the entire family. We even began to teach on Sundays to their family and other families that joined us at their home. Then we went to other homes, and more families joined us.
Finally, a church in the next neighborhood opened their doors to us,

and we joined their church family. During all this time we were helping them get their papers and visas so they could work and drive legally.

We taught them about the Love of Jesus. Some made a profession of faith in Christ. We married them, we visited their families in Mexico, then we moved out of state. But the relationship continued. They have come to visit us almost every year.

They just visited, and Maria is pregnant with her third child, a little boy. She already has two fine boys.

When her life gets hard sometimes, she still reaches out, and she knows I will always point her to Jesus. She already knows He's the answer, but just needs confirmation.

Lupe –

Lupe and Maria are cousins. Maria's mom and Lupe's dad are brother and sister. Lupe's family was also a big part of our ministry in Center Hill, FL. Lupe's brothers and sisters, as well as mom and dad were a part of our gatherings for worship in the yards of the families in Center Hill.

I was involved in many aspects of her family's life. We also visited her grandfather and her mom's sisters in Mexico. Their work did not have the same parameters as Maria's so we were not as involved with their visas and papers. We helped with schooling and food. We tried to get them involved in a local church, but there was none in the local town that they could go to. That's why our home church began at her auntie's house.

With both families we were and remain good friends. Even the extended families in Mexico keep us up to date with their joys and sorrows. Prayer is still a big part of our involvement.

Here's one of those "God things" that He does when you are connected. I believe this is the Power of Holy Spirit in action.
Lupe's family had gone to California to build greenhouses – her

father, her brothers and sister – and one day out of the blue she called me. This is five years after we had moved to South Carolina. Her family had been in California for about that same amount of time.

She wanted to ask how I was doing and how Mr. John, my husband, was doing, and then she wanted to just talk a little bit. What she kept saying over and over was how important it is to forgive family when they aren't very nice or speak unkindly. "You know, they are family and you really love them and they love you, and you have to forgive them. They don't really mean it." she said.

The irony of it all was that I was having a hard time forgiving one of my family members and she was preaching to me and didn't even know it. Finally, I said, "Lupe, The Lord had you call me and tell me that He wanted me to forgive my family member." "You have just told me what He has tried to tell me, but I didn't want to." "Now it's funny and it's easy to do when there a little humor in it."

She laughed and I thanked her. I don't know if she ever really understood what her call meant to me, but God knows.

Dr. Nicku Kyungu Mordi

Today I spoke with a friend, Dr. Nicku Kyungu Mordi. She asked how I was doing, and I told her about the book The Lord has asked me to write about children.

I told her the scriptures given to me as a foundational statement, and the belief I have, that infants can know the Lord and learn the scriptures for their destiny and purpose on the earth. She said she had something to share about that and gave me permission to share her words in my book.

She said, "Yes. When her children were in the womb, she would say the Lord's Prayer with them but when she was tired, she would put a tape recorder on her tummy for the child to continue to hear the Lord's Prayer. After they were born, and were able to talk some, when she prayed, they would just finish the sentence prayer after she started. They were very little and they already knew the prayer."

Then she shared a scripture the Lord gave her when her children were babes: **Psalm 8:2**. *"Out of the mouth of babes and nursing infants You have ordained strength, Because of Your enemies, That You may silence the enemy and the avenger"* **(Psalms 8:2 NKJV).**

I think I like the Message Bible version of this scripture the best. Listen to this: *"Nursing infants gurgle choruses about YOU; toddlers shout the songs That drown out enemy talk, and silence atheist babble"*
(Psalm 8:2 MSG). Amen.

Isn't this just oh so wonderfully true?

I have introduced the importance of American Christian children understanding the governmental Covenant we have with our nation. The value I found in teaching American Christian History Curriculum presents the Providential movement of men and nations; not only Americans have the Providential movement of God on men and nations, but all nations. Dr. Nicku Kyungu Mordi was moved by God to sound the alarm of united prayers for nations and declare America for Jesus and Africa for Jesus as well as praying for presidents of nations to have good governance *(Prov. 29:2)*. This was witnessed in her original nation of Tanzania, Africa when the former president John Magufuli brought transformation to his nation.

Her faith inspired the Body of Christ to same day unity prayers and contact with the former President of Tanzania, which moved him to declare national prayer days that brought hope and peace. Also Dr. Mordi's simple teachings on sustainable strategies to change communities caused the President to enforce hard work that helped him to stand in faith to fight corruption to promote prosperity and health to the people of Tanzania, particularly during the COVID 19 pandemic.

I would like to recommend two books my friend Dr. Mordi wrote that tell of her life experiences with the Lord as a young girl that formed a great faith in her to trust the Lord for miracles – miracles that affected lives in Sweden, Norway, and Russia, and the governmental leadership of her home nation, Tanzania, Africa.

My Recommendations

The following two books are a must read for the parents, guardians or teachers of the next generation of the Children of God:

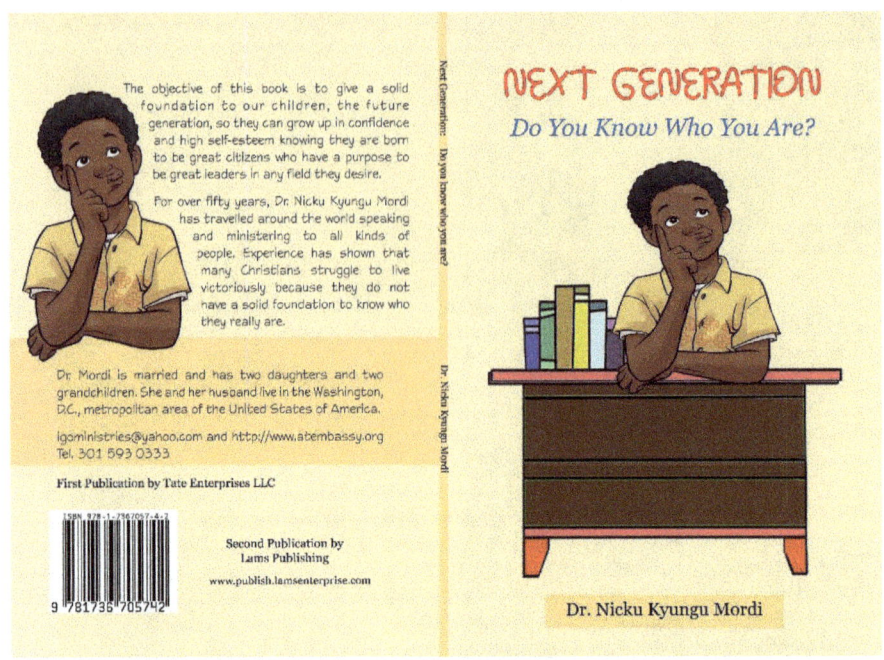

Chapter 12 – I Met an Angel Today and Other Testimonies

Gabriel

I met an angel today. His name was Gabriel, just like the one in the Bible.

He was struggling in his earth suit. The tone of his voice was strained and high pitched. He was really having a hard time.

It was hard to listen to. His mom took him out to settle him down, but the sound continued. My heart ached for him.

A little later I headed out toward the restrooms, and at the spur of the moment went up to Gabriel, surprising him and myself, and put my hand on his head and said, "Peace, be still. Receive the peace of the Lord."

Immediately his straining stopped and he smiled. His mom said tell the nice lady thank you. I said, "No Gabriel, thank Jesus." With a sweet, childlike response he said, "Tank Jeedsus".

It was from then on I could see the joy of Gabriel in his earth suit. I haven't seen him for a while. I wonder if he's got his wings. ☺

This is another time where my touch, on Gabriel's head in this instance, was the touch of Holy Spirit FIRE power, or now I can even call it the healing virtue of the Lord Jesus. They are both dunamis power for kingdom living.

Three Angels

The leader said, "Ok, see the lady in the green sweater? There are three angels over her head. They have come to heal. Just put your hand on her."

I looked around for the lady in the green sweater, and it was me.

I wasn't sure what to do. I really wanted to run, but that would have been selfish since he said the angels were dispensing the healing of God through me. I stayed, as hands touched me. I then touched a man sitting right in from of me as the leader prayed.

Two things I take away from this encounter with angels.

1. The angels did not only come to heal, but to anoint in power for ministry. The man I was praying for said he felt such power in his arms. They were like turbine engines and if he aimed them at the wall across the room, the wall would fall down like the walls of Jericho. This had to be an example of Holy Spirit FIRE power.

In the devotional, "Streams In The Desert", November 13, page 426, A. B. Simpson writes, "God is looking for people on whom He can place the weight of His entire love, power, and faithful promises. And His engines are strong enough to pull any weight we may attach to them. She is referencing Genesis 18:19. "God chose Abraham because He knew he would direct his children in the things of God." The KJV says it differently but the meaning is the same. It uses the word "command" instead of "direct". Command is a primitive root that means to intensively constitute. Constitute is a verb that means to set, to fix, to form or compose; to give formal existence to; to make a thing what it is. *"Truth and reason constitute that intellectual gold that defies destruction."* (Noah Webster's 1828 American Dictionary).

As the devotion has said, the power of God was being demonstrated in Abraham for the ministry God was raising him up to do. It would require the greatest faith and determination, love and strength of purpose to accomplish it.

The man I prayed for had been called by God to go into the nations and train young men to be Christian leaders. He had developed a new curriculum and philosophy of education. It would require of him the same faith and determination, love and strength of purpose to accomplish what God had called him to do. Last I heard he was doing just that in an amazing display of the favor and power of God.

2. As we were ending the prayer time a man and his son came into the room. The son was pulling his dad and the leader knew the father and son. He said, "I'm not surprised. You brought (his son) to see the angels."

Here was a small boy who came from the front of the conference center, which was quite a distance away, to see angels. I wondered how he knew angels were there. He wasn't even close to our area. As I listened to the father and the leader speak together it became clear that this little boy was able to see into the spirit realm and was part of a prayer team in their school.

This was a place where the leadership had discovered the authority of God to heal and know the signs of the times like the tribe of Issachar in the young children. They had developed a program to help the parents encourage the children in their sight and hearing. They already knew about what I am only just now able to understand, and it was going on that day. That school was getting children ready to fly because the Kingdom is coming in power.

Later one of the women who came with us said a little girl came over to her in the balcony when she was praying and laid her hand on her and prayed in the Spirit for her. The woman did not know the little girl, but the little girl said God wanted to heal her so she came to pray. That simple and that complete. The woman was healed.

There is a scripture in the Bible that says children have their own angels that are before the face of God in their behalf *(Matthew 18: 10-11)*, and you better think twice before you do anything harmful to even one of them.

No wonder the children know what's happening in the Spirit. Their angels get information right from the mouth of God for them. I was looking on the web and found an article written by a woman who studied babies that were newborn. She said up to 3 months babies can see images beyond our reality up to two feet away.

She didn't say it was heaven, but she did say it was spiritual images. I believe the innocence of the babies born of the will of God are able to bring heaven to earth.

For many generations adults have believed, even if they didn't say it out loud, "Children are to be seen and not heard." That is a lie we must correct.

Jacob

Blue eyed towhead with charisma. Front and center and full of life. That is how I would describe this little man filled with energy and curiosity. He was a good student, and would really push it when there was the least competition from one of the other boys.

Both were as sweet as could be, but occasionally I could almost see them nose to nose trying to be the best, quickest, quietest, and first at something. They kept each other on their toes. Every classroom needs a little friendly competition, and my class had that two years in a row.

Jacob was in my class both years. He was a joy to have in the room. His friends were in my class as well and we had a family atmosphere.

One of the subjects I taught was Bible. One lesson was about "forgiving and loving your enemy." I had just passed out our worksheet and our Bibles. The assignment was on the board, so I asked one of the students to read the instructions out loud to the rest of the class. ***Matthew 5: 43-44***: *"But I say unto you, love your enemies, bless them that curse you, do good to them that hate you,* *and pray for them which despitefully use you, and persecute you;"*

About that time Jacob raised his hand and asked me, "Mrs. Mapp, does God love Satan and does He forgive him?"

I was stopped dead in my tracks.

I said, "Jacob, that's a very good question." I thought to myself "Jesus is our example, so it would seem He does love Satan and would forgive him, but I can't recall ever seeing that in scripture." I wasn't sure if Satan was already condemned to the pit, or if God had not given up on him, or what. So, I told Jacob I'd have to get back to him about that later. And we continued with our lesson.

I did do some research and did ask a few more knowledgeable than myself, but I didn't like their answers. The God I was getting to know would not have responded the way those I asked responded. So I let it go and Jacob did not ask me again…that year.

The next year we were studying the Bible and the same scripture, regarding loving your enemy and praying and forgiving them, came round again.

And … Jacob's hand went up and he asked, "Mrs. Mapp, does Jesus love His enemy Satan and does He pray for him and forgive him?" Here we go again, and I was ashamed to tell Jacob I still did not have an answer I was sure of. I knew what the Bible said about the responsibility of teachers for their words.

So, once again I told Jacob I still wasn't sure about that and I'd get back with him as soon as I knew.

The year ended and I did not teach at that school after that year. I kept up with Jacob through his mom's Facebook for a while. Thirteen years later I got a card in the mail. The timing of that card was divinely orchestrated. Here's the story:

It was Sunday morning and my husband and I were off to church. I really liked this small church. The pastor would allow questions during his message if we didn't understand something.

This Sunday the sermon was from the book of Matthew, chapter 5. I smiled to myself as the pastor began. He spent most of his time on the Beatitudes, but then he moved quickly to the end of the chapter, which was where Jacob's question was waiting for an answer. So when the pastor asked if there were any questions, I raised my hand.

I said, "I've got a question for you. I had a little student in my classroom two years in a row. We studied these scriptures and both years he asked me the same question and both years I told him I'd have to get back with him. Here's the question. When the scripture says love your enemies and pray for them and forgive them, does Jesus love Satan and pray for him and forgive him?" This is the question of a four- and five-year-old."

The pastor looked at me shook his head and smiled. Then he asked if anyone in the auditorium would like to answer. No one raised their hand and a few were smiling. Then he asked Melinda, one of the worship team members. She answered in such a way that, all of a sudden, the light came on. She said, "Jesus would forgive Satan, but Satan would never ask."

I had never even considered the arrogance of Satan, but when she said it so matter-of-factly, I saw it. I went to her after church and thanked her. I told her this was a question that had gone unanswered for years.

On our way home we stopped at the mailbox to get yesterday's mail and there was Jacob's letter in the mailbox. A graduation card from Jacob. I was sooooo excited. I finally had an answer to his question and he had written, so I had a current address to respond to.

Later that evening as I pondered the answer given at church, the Lord expanded my understanding. He said, "The most powerful WORD of God, Jesus, was taken into the devil's territory by the greatest convicter of hearts, Holy Spirit, and in the loving Presence of God the Father, but the devil just walked away." Just like Melinda said, "the devil walked away unchanged."

So I sent a graduation card with the answer to Jacob's question and a graduation gift. His mom texted when Jacob told her I had written. She thanked me and said he was tickled. Thirteen years not a word, then on the day I had an answer a card comes. That is sooooo God.

Chapter 13 - Forever Children

We are forever and always children of God. From before we are born into the earth until we return to Him, we are His children. His relationship to us changes as we mature, but we are forever His children.

This chapter is about the adults that even as children never learned The Love of the FATHER. I was one of those children until the chronological age of 27. He came for me. He awakened His Holy Spirit in me and put FIRE on my head. I became young again.

I can't explain it, but the awakening of His Spirit in me changed me from the inside out. Restored Innocence is one way I understand what happened. I did a painting of the lion with the lamb and called it "Restored Innocence." I have it hanging on my art gallery wall of children I have painted.

As a Christian I have the opportunity to meet other Christian women and in so many cases I am speaking a different language even to them about my relationship with Jesus. One day while praying I realized I was in the Throne Room of God. He said to me, as He pointed away from Himself, *"See My Son."*

It took me some time to understand, but I now believe He was giving me Sight. The ability to see the things of God, in the Spirit. Or another way to say that is, to see things the way He sees them.

Since that time, I often am aware of the heart of the matter, even beyond words, when talking with other women or children or even men. He gives me understanding and words to express His heart to them. Sometimes the understanding of what I said doesn't come until a little later.

As I begin this chapter, I am going to look at the importance of knowing our identity in Christ. If as a child we never knew who Jesus says we are, or that He loves us very much, it changes who we become. We doubt our abilities, we doubt our importance to Him or to others. We are uncertain of our purpose and we live way under the possibilities we are created with.

I am still learning that. This book is an expression of the decision to launch out and write what He said He has put in me to write. There is little confidence, but there is the knowing that obedience releases a blessing – for me, and for those who need to hear what I have to say.

For the forever children I want to say, we have an inheritance from The Lord Jesus. The fact that He died for us brings us into the highest court to hear what is written on the will and testament of Our Heavenly Father.

We receive all that He died to give us, because He loved us so much that He would die to give us what we lost in the Garden of our creation, which was all things, and most importantly, a relationship with Father, a big Family, and an amazing identity.

Ok, so now I can't express enough the importance of having Holy Spirit as our constant companion. He leads us into all truth. He helps us remove the blinders, cobwebs, and veils from whatever is blocking the knowledge of the Love of God for each of us. His FIRE burns it all away.

If we know who we are and the liberty in which we stand in Christ we will not be fooled by the lies of the enemy in our individual lives, relationships, community and world. Earlier I mentioned how important it is to understand the principles revealed in the liberty of Christ. They are being stolen from us at every level of life and we don't even know it.

Jesus knows and is calling to me, and to us, to "Protect the Children." He is showing me what that protection will look like, and it will require the FIRE of Holy Spirit to reveal what He has put in each one to take back what the enemy has stolen, not only for our children but for the generations that follow.

This has become an exercise in obedience for me. So to "Protect the Children" as in my dream I was not to worry about a Tea Kettle with spots. I had begun to think, "I am not a clean vessel. I still have spots, (or besetting sin)." But God said to me, "I have taken care of the spots; you must protect the children. The water must always be hot, and only a few can help you."

Then He showed me an image for the "cleansing flow." A picture of the water from the altar and the blood from the cross flowing out of sight and filled with every guilt and shame I have ever had or that I will ever have. It is gone in the "cleansing flow," and not just me, but all who come to the throne or the cross to be cleansed.

It is the lie of the enemy to tell anyone they are too big a sinner or too messed up or too anything for him to forgive, save, heal, and deliver. I remember finding a scripture when the kids were little that said *"...He is able to deliver to the uttermost those who come to God through Him, since He ever lives to make intercession for them"* **(Hebrews 7:25)**. Totally amazing, and to some "preposterous," but totally TRUE.

I think some of us have gotten confused with the rest of the scripture. It has been taught that because He is Holy, He is separate – so much higher and holier than sinners that He is untouchable. That is the lie. Check out **Zephaniah 3:17**. Now that's the truth. He's holding on to us and singing over us, even whispering His love in our ear.

This poem turned into a hymn says it:

Oh the deep deep love of Jesus, vast unmeasured boundless free. Rolling as a mighty ocean, in His fullness over me.

Underneath me, all around me, is the current of His love. Leading onward leading homeward to Thy glorious rest above.

Oh the deep deep love of Jesus, spread His praise from shore to shore. How He Loveth, ever Loveth, changes never, never more.

How He watch o'er His loved ones, died to call them all His own. How for them He intercedeth, watches over them from the throne.

Oh, the deep deep love of Jesus, Love of every love the best: "Tis an ocean vast of blessing, 'Tis a haven sweet of rest. Oh the deep deep love of Jesus, 'Tis a heav'n of heav'ns to me; And it lifts me up to glory, for it lifts me up to Thee.

(Samuel Trevor Francis 1834-1925) originally wrote the words to this Hymn as a poem in a publication in 1898. In his preface he included this explanation:

Many of these poems have appeared in various religious and semi-religious papers and magazines. The author has collected them together and with others which have never before seen the light, launches them forth on their message. If he has touched upon the sorrows and the dark side of human life, he has endeavoured to show how light, hope, and joy may be found. He trusts that those poems that are hymn-like will not be altered to suit the whims or theology of hymn-book compilers. This book is not written in the interests of any sect, denomination, or party, but for all who "love our Lord Jesus Christ in sincerity and truth."

I understand why Jesus said in many and diverse ways, we come to him as little children - only as a child will we be able to enter the kingdom of God.

This is not a reprimand. This is a fact. Children come into this world innocent. They then learn who they are in this world. All too often they are told awful lies about themselves – some on purpose and some without malice.

I believe they know fully well who they are in the eternal world, where God lives, but when they come here, we are given the wonderful task of opening up that treasure in their lives.

I have been called to protect that truth in His children. The complete uncovering of the meaning of the word "protect" is WHO HE IS. His very nature. He is our protector and He made that very clear in *(Deuteronomy 32:38)*. If you read the entire chapter, you will see HE is mocking the ability of any other false god to protect His children.

Now, through the SON of God, who is divine and human, we are told in Matthew to go and do everything Jesus said, and Holy Spirit will reveal from HIM what we weren't ready to hear, but which is now needed *(John 16:12-13)*. I call that Providence.

So as I look at the definition of "Protect" I am struck with the knowing that every word describes the nature of God. If I am to "Protect" the Children then I must be as He Is in the Earth. I Am in Christ and have His new nature. A new creation in Christ NOW.

WHAT DOES THAT LOOK LIKE? It is the nature of God in me, in each one of us.

To Keep - It means to hedge about, to guard, attend # H8104 and #H2421, to live, to revive, preserve, quicken.

To Safeguard- #H 4931 - custody, watch over, safe.

To Shield - #H4043 - (or buckler), protector, defense.

To Preserve - #H 2421 - to live, make alive, nourish, quicken, repair, make alive.

To Shelter - #H 4268 - hope, place of refuge, trust.

To Guard - #H 7323 - footman, runner; #H 4928 - superiority in mental action.

To Watch over - #H 6822 - lean toward, keep; #H 821 - peer into the distance.

To Mount - #H 2021 - position of advantage, (fig.) promotion.

To Refuge - #H 4585 - habitation, dwelling place; #H 4733 - taking in.

To Secure - #H 982 - to trust, be confident, make to hope, place of refuge.

To Deliver - #H 5414 - to give, appoint, bestow, assign, charge, send, restore.

When I looked up these words there were two that really stood out to me personally. To Deliver is the word "Nathan" in Hebrew. Nathan is the name of our son and the description of the word describes him.

The other one was the word To Secure. It was used in the scripture *(Job 11:18)* and the story line in *Job 11* was a discourse with Zophar, who tells Job he should put away wickedness and put iniquity far away, then will he (Job) lift up his face without spot to God. Later in the book of Job God reprimands Zophar. He silences him for speaking what he doesn't know and tells Job to pray for him and two others.

The reason this spoke to me is because God told me not to worry about the "spots" on my tea kettle. He said He would take care of them. Seeing that story in Job confirmed God's word to me. Spots are God's job, not mine, and not Job's.

Chapter 14 – Transference

Wow, Baby Jesus filled Elizabeth and John with the power of the Holy Spirit while HE was in Mary's Womb. Could that possibly be the truth that God wants me to bring as a protection for the children.

As I share this with my science minded husband, he says, "I need more proof before I can believe it is even possible." I said, "OK," and the Lord said to me, "Transference."

I didn't begin investigating what transference meant right away. The thought of being a new creation in Christ has always meant to me that everything is transformed into the image of a resurrected Christ. As **2 Corinthians 5: 17-20** says, *"If any man be in Christ, he is a new creation. Old things pass away ALL things become new..."*

So why wouldn't it be possible for Jesus to transform John in the womb? My reasoning did not impress my husband so I began to see what a more scientific approach might be. I hoped to find an answer that might be possible.

I remember reading a book by Perry Marshall about Evolution and the genetic structure of man and man's many transformations through history. His book is "Evolution 2.0," and it is a fresh look at evolution that is scientifically based, yet not hostile to the Christian faith. It differs from the random mutation plus natural selection

Darwinian version which is the orthodox version of evolution accepted by scientists.

I thought I'd see if Perry Marshall had anything to say about transference, since I knew my husband agreed scientifically with Perry Marshall on the matter of evolution. He did not have the word transference in his index in the back, but his description of epigenetics and Genome Duplication combined are reminiscent of what happened to Elizabeth and John in the presence of the Son of God while in Mary's womb. "...Epigenetics controls the expression of every cell in the human body" (p. 115). "It is also primarily a tool of fine-tuning and gradual adaptation over multiple generations. But in concert with Genome Duplication...it becomes an agent of massive change and high-speed progress" (p. 119).

I wanted to find a definition of the word transference.

Transference-the act of transferring or the process of being transferred. That's Oxford Dictionary, and I would say that hardly explains it. I must look a little farther. Merriam-Webster uses another word to describe it: conveyance – The act of bearing, carrying or transporting; transmitting, or transferring from one person to another.

mannaexpressonline.com presents an article about 13 ways transference of Spirit happens. This is more in line with theology/religion than science, but it is something I personally experienced, so that puts it in the category of observational evidence.

One of the 13 ways of spiritual transference was through the TV. The author said that the viewer of the show could receive something spiritual by watching a TV show. I know this might sound ridiculous to many, but to me it was truth. I received a new meniscus in my right knee. I had torn the meniscus in the back of my right knee and the orthopedic surgeon said there is nothing he could do other than go in and remove the debris. There is no procedure presently approved or known that repairs a meniscus.

I had talked to others who had that procedure and they were still having problems so I said "no thanks." Shortly after that I was walking by my TV at home and a pastor from Bethel Church in Redding, California said the Lord was doing something different. He was performing creative miracles. He is giving a new meniscus to whoever needs one. I was amazed so I walked up to the TV and said, "I need one," and I got one. Ta-daaaaaa.

I won't go over all the other ways, but there are two more I have experienced. One was what I call The Gabriel effect which I talked about in chapter 11. The other was when the Holy Spirit just began to heal my spine by causing my body to sway back and forth. I'm not sure what that is called.

Now, let's look at what Perry Marshall has to say and see if there are any scientific models to match what happened to Elizabeth and John.

Marshall gives an example of the concept of transposition on page 87 in his book. He relates it to Barbara McClintock's corn transposition where the cells of the corn displayed what he called a "mutation algorithm," which I am calling a "glorious algorithm" because the cell made the smarter substitution to accommodate the needed change in the corn. Perry related his explanation to the need of a giraffe to have a longer neck to reach the tree tops for food, so the cells "mutated" to accommodate the new condition of its environment and it didn't take year upon year which would be random mutation's answer.

This might be a reach for some, but if we Christians believe we are a new creation in Christ and we are NOW seated with Him in heavenly places, we have moved up, just as the head of the giraffe grew up to accommodate the new condition. Its cells mutated and our DNA was made new by our new location, in Christ. We have "put on the new life, which is renewed in knowledge after the pattern in which it was originally created" (***Colossians 3:10, Aramaic***).

Marshall wanted to get to the bottom of the mutation algorithm vs. random mutation, so he decided to study and look for honest proof about the "mutation algorithm" vs. random selection algorithm which takes many millennia. On page 310 his final answer was, "Empiricism [which] showed [him] that all codes whose origins we know have been designed, (not random). Empiricism [also] said evolving codes always obey layers of linguistic rules." Did you know our genes talk to each other? They do.

When looking at creation or any part of the creation model, the vantage point of the recorder matters for our understanding. He believes much of the creation account is from earth's vantage point.

My vantage point seems to be moving higher and higher so that what I record in my book might seem ridiculous or even impossible to believe or understand. I am moving into the unknown and I agree with Marshall. He cited the scripture, *"It is the glory of God to conceal a matter and the glory of kings to search it out"* **(Proverbs 22:4)**. EXACTLY.

What I am suggesting as a plan to protect the children is from God's perspective. It is new understanding for me. His work is finished and his time frame is eternal. Earth's perspective is unfolding and time is linear.

In the Appendix 2 of the book, on page 315, Marshall offered a comparison chart of the Genesis account with a science interpretation for each scripture.

Q – What is man *(Genesis 1:26-27)*? *"Man is a spiritual being, the first creature made in God's image. Unlike the animals, man is body and spirit. This is why the origin of man's body plan, which is adapted from lower animals, doesn't alter his spirit identity as a child of God."*

He says *"the unfolding of meaning to 'Our Story' as written in the Bible has relied on the relationship of God to man and through the prophets. (God always tells His prophets before He does anything" (Amos 3:7)*.

Perry Marshall makes a statement on page 320, and it resonates with me and even points to the possibility of my proposal of Holy Spirit baptism in the womb.

Under his sub-heading "Was there pain, suffering and death before the Fall?," he points out that *"most evangelicals widely believe the early Earth was perfect and Adam and Eve introduced death into the world. This belief is based on **Romans 5:12**, '...just as sin entered the world through one man, and death through sin...therefore all sinned.'"*

But he says, *"read the rest of Romans 5 with care. What kind of death is Paul talking about? Notice,*
in ***Romans 5:17-18***, *'For if by one man's offence death reigned by one; much more they which receive abundance of grace and of the gift of righteousness shall reign in life by one, Jesus Christ. Therefore as by the offence of one, judgment came upon all men to condemnation; even so by the righteous act of one the free gift came upon all men unto justification of life.'"*

Death is defeated by life. Is he talking about physical death or spiritual death? In both cases he is talking about spiritual death in humanity. There was no mention of plants or animals in this death/life scenario.

Marshall says there is no mention of a perfect paradise in this garden (it was staffed by a very clever serpent from the word go, was it not?). The tree of life was the only mention of immortality.

It's hard for some conservative Christians to believe God created a world that has suffering as part of humanity's process, but scripture reveals suffering is part:

- *"Some take the Kingdom by force and the kingdom suffers violence"* – ***Matthew 11:12***.

- Jesus speaks of being persecuted for righteousness' sake – ***Matthew 5:10***

- Paul speaks of having to enter the kingdom through much persecution – ***Acts 14:22***

Just to name a few.

Ok- according to the scientific interpretation of scripture ***Genesis 2:23, "Being made in the image of God changes not only the way we see ourselves, but our relationship to others"*** (page 328)
Soooo, there can be observable evidence that "born again" believers, are made in the image of God. They have changed in measurable ways.

There is another scientific consideration Marshall mentions on page 135, Chapter 16. It is called Punctuated Equilibrium, which states that if organisms can radically reorganize their own DNA in one generation, then evolution might happen very rapidly... but only under certain conditions.

Another evolutionary theory that was studied in the 1970's was Genome Duplication. I am not a scientist, but the way it is described in summary by Marshall sounds like the duplication of genomes fueled sudden, radical transformation of body plans. It explained how, in a few exceedingly rare events the genetic chassis for new species could be built suddenly.

It sounds like another interesting possibility in Punctuated Equilibrium, which existed where the original pattern of genomes lay unchanged until a sudden force acted upon them and they resurfaced in a newer stronger pattern.

That is science talk. This is my theological explanation.

We were created in the image of God. We sinned against Him and lost the spiritual part of our original design pattern. Then Jesus came and restored us to our original pattern, and suddenly we were even better than we were before. The original pattern had been deactivated, our Spirit Power was considered dead, and now we are Spirit beings as well as flesh beings once again, and the makeup of our soul is back to its original pattern.

If it's true that through Adam comes "spiritual death," and all are born spiritually dead with no Holy Spirit "dunamis power" – power necessary to maneuver out of the grasp of Satan – wouldn't it be just like our Creator to have put something in us – An innate ability to

receive dunamis power in the womb to repel the enemy from our inception?
Couldn't it be that what God the Holy Spirit put in Mary, and then Mary transferred to Jesus, and then Jesus did for Elizabeth and John, is the answer for what is needed today to protect the children of our generation and the next?

A Holy Spirit and FIRE before they receive a water baptism. Or, from the vantage point of Heaven, a baptism in the Spirit like the original pattern of our design, and then the added water baptism from earth's perspective to bury the old Adamic nature.

That would yield a generation of Holy Spirit filled kids that are hidden in Christ in God and the enemy wouldn't want to mess with those kids, because they know "who's their Daddy." They become the untouchable.

So let's look at transference from the beginning of time. It is recorded in scripture that Adam's sin reigned, ruled in all humanity, until the One Man's righteous act…came to all men. I call that transferring onto all humanity the sin of Adam. And on the other hand, I call what Jesus did as the transference of righteousness, resulting in justification to all men.

The Bible puts a future condition on the ruling of righteousness in all mankind, but there was no condition on what Adam did to transfer his sin.

Interesting, don't you think?

Here's another thought regarding transference from Adam. What Adam transferred to us was only temporary. Once Christ came on the scene and accomplished His complete obedience at the Cross in real time, His act was an act that is inalienable. Totally impossible to undo – nothing temporary about it.

We have even been created to accept this sudden reversal physically as well as spiritually from death to life, which is an inalienable gift. Although the physical body will die, the spirit and soul live on. And the physical can receive extended life, or healing or deliverance, that is considered supernatural by many but really is natural to the new life in Christ.

In Ungers Bible Dictionary on page 1112, the word "translate" is the act of transferring something. It is explained as a word in both Hebrew and Greek that has the sense of removal of a person or thing from one state or condition to another.

If I look up "translate(d)" in Strong's I found only two scriptures: **Colossians 1:13** and **Hebrews 11:5**.

In the Colossians scripture: *"who hath delivered us from the power of darkness, and hath translated* us into the kingdom of his dear Son" (Colossians 1:13)*. In my NKJV Nelson Open Bible translation the asterisk indicates the word "transferred" is translated - #G3179, to transfer.

The **Hebrew 11:5** scripture: *"By faith Enoch was translated that he should not see death; and was not found, because God had translated him: for before his translation he had this testimony, that he pleased God."* translated - #G3346, to transfer.

Another use of the word in Unger's book was found in **2 Samuel 3:10**: *"to translate the kingdom from the house of Saul, and to set up the throne of David over Israel and over Judah, from Dan even to Beer-Sheba."* It was the transferring of a kingdom from one to another.

I don't believe this is a stretch, but some might. Isn't what happened to Elizabeth and John at the sound of Mary's voice and the filling of the Holy Spirit the same as being transferred from the kingdom of darkness to the kingdom of light? That's what Jesus does for us as we accept His gift of salvation. And then we even receive the baptism of the Holy Spirit to live victoriously on the earth even as we are in heaven with the Lord. Hid with God in Christ. Jesus lived His victorious life in the power of the Spirit and told His disciples to wait for the promise from on high in order to live their life victoriously in the fulfilling of His Command to go and make disciples of all nations. We go with the message of the Gospel. They receive the Gospel message, and then We baptize them – but wait, there's more – and then send the Holy Spirit power and FIRE into their lives to live their new life with an anointing that breaks the yoke of slavery.

I have another story about Holy Spirit power transferring life into a dead womb. My cousin was visiting Texas and she was out to dinner with friends from a local church. The elder of the church was there with his family and it was his daughter and her husband that had been trying to get pregnant for a while.

My cousin suddenly stood up, raised her hand and declared, "You will have a baby." Then she sat back down and was shocked at herself and confused (it was like she was out of time and then returned).

One of her first thoughts was, "What have I done?" Everyone looked at her, but then just went on with ordering. It scared her to death she said and she hoped she never did that again.

Here is some of her back story. She is the wife of a deceased Presbyterian pastor. At that time, she had only been actively practicing her Spiritual prayer language for a few hours. She woke up in the night and began to pray in tongues. She had never done that before. Now it feels more natural for her to pray in tongues. At church she sits in the balcony and sings in tongues and speaks in tongues when the Apostles Creed is repeated.

This is something much like the Mary and Elizabeth encounter. By the way, the young girl and her husband had a baby that next year. Very interesting.

Chapter 15 – Agency / Agencies

As I said earlier in my book, I introduced the foundational points of my book to a pastor friend who is also a well-studied Bible Scholar. As he listened to the elementary principles I'm introducing in my book – which are self-government, individuality, Christian character, and conscience being the most sacred property – he responded by saying, "That's agency."

He asked who my target audience will be and I said, "parents, teachers and guardians – adults mostly. The key point is really teaching children how to understand the importance of government – not political party government but rather who you will allow to rule, control, or lead you, and how will you control yourself, rule your passions and temper, and lead others."

Again, he said, "What you're talking about is 'agency.'" So, I'm introducing that because I only learned and studied government at a secondary school level and then applied what I learned to the adult life I'm living. Agency was not a word used in the children's curriculum, but it is a word mature adults would understand because it means:

"Agency - The quality of moving or of exerting power; the state of being in action; action; operation; instrumentality; as, the agency of providence in the natural world." **Webster 1828 American Dictionary, Noah Webster**

When the rights of an individual are taken away and one is forced to respond contrary to their conscience, that is taking away their agency. What I hope my children learned, and what I hope to teach the parents of other children, is that our government and the government of God are all about knowing one has the authority to choose according to the dictates of their own heart, a heart ruled by Christ in the Holy Spirit power.

So he understood at an adult level what I was saying at a child's level. Children need to know this so that when a government or other is trying to force a response that they disagree with, they can say "no."

He recommended I get a clear understanding of what Jesus meant when He said, "to enter the Kingdom of God you must be like a little child."

What did Jesus mean? Most of what the pastor has read about this scripture was that Jesus was referring to the innocence of the child, but he doesn't believe babies are innocent when born. They are of Adam and thus sinners. So it couldn't be innocence, at least the way he understands innocence.

Well, if Adam's sin is imputed automatically to everyone born under heaven, then Jesus's saving grace is imputed to everyone born under heaven, yet man puts a condition on the receiver of that grace. Not sure about that.

Here's a scientific answer, compliments of Mr. John Mapp, Jr.

"Newton's first law: 'Objects at rest will stay at rest unless acted upon by an outside force. Objects in motion will remain in motion unless acted upon by an outside force.' Adam's choice set humanity on a trajectory. That trajectory will continue unchanged unless we make a different choice in order to change our course. Thanks to the work of Jesus, all we have to do to change course is believe in Him."

So, as it is seen from heaven, or from the mind of God, Jesus was that object that acted upon the trajectory of sin, setting another course of righteousness, peace and joy in the Holy Spirit. All creation is in the flow of the new life in Christ from Gods reference point. But Paul said all we need to do is believe on Him, whom HE, meaning God the Father, sent. But the flow is flowing even if you don't believe yet.

Here's another observation: the fact that children have their very own angels before the face of God in their behalf *(Matthew 18:10)* – is it not an indication of their innocence? I don't know for sure, but it seems so to me.

Think about a new baby. All they can do is trust. Every need they have for life is dependent on another. Even in the womb they were dependent on the mother for food. As they grow, they experience the life around them and they respond and adapt to what is around them based on what already exists within them. I don't think it is exclusively outward influence or inward heredity. I believe they work together to form the whole.

They form what we call a personality. Oh, the joy of that first smile, or that first sound. Crying is a language they use to tell us of their need or discomfort. As they continue to mature, they are most courageous. They must learn to see, speak, understand, and respond to certain impulses, and learn how to communicate.

In the individual formation of who they are we can see laughter, delight, wonder, energy, and curiosity. And as they continue to grow, they learn to relate to others with kindness, quick forgiveness, laughter, exploration of the new, and fearlessness toward their new world.

That said, all that is beautiful in a newborn and infant and toddler and child can be stolen from them by evil minded individuals – slave traffickers and sex traders to name a few.

Why would children be the preferred target of evil-minded men? Is it because of their innocence that man says they don't have, but God says they do? Guess who is out to steal from God everything He loves. That's right, Satan is after the innocence of our children. So, if they aren't innocent what is this all about?

They, the children, are seen as precious and innocent by God, and what the kingdom is about. And they are being stolen because they are precious and innocent.

Rescue Agencies

Today I decided to venture into the information reported on the internet regarding sex trafficking and slave labor, and found human trafficking to be the most commonly used heading for information.

I was totally surprised. I knew numbers were high, but charts and graphs were presented by government agencies that were head shakingly unbelievable. I'm not going to present any of that information in this book, but if you are curious just go on line and you can find any number of articles, reports, agencies, etc. with information. The number of children is staggering.

Something I did notice in ALL the reports I checked, which was limited I confess, not one single Christian organization was recognized as "other than government" assistance in the articles. I will include a few of the global charts just for visual understanding of the size of the problem.

It is God-sized. I know the Christian agencies and ministries bring God into the mix by the sheer fact that Christ is in them and they are in Christ. Also, the power of Holy Spirit is active in their efforts too. Their victories are not loudly publicized because anonymity is crucial.

I have not contacted any Christian organization for updated information about their efforts to rescue the children in the trafficking industry. Yes, it is an industry, a huge money-making industry. Human life is devalued as far as respecting their individual personhood, but valued as chattel, merchandise for profit.

As I've said all along, only God can protect. He said so in the scriptures. He mocked our choice of any source of protection other than Himself. My friend, we are at the point of depravity of mind and heart that requires the greatest heart change. The heart of man is desperately wicked and only God can change that. He already has provided Who we need. His name is Jesus and He is the only Savior of the world. He has been from the beginning, and has made all things and is overseeing His creation.

The decision to choose His heart for how we live is ours. It is not clear to me how we can continue on this road of depravity and live. He is our answer. Government is not the answer, and we have abdicated responsibility to government all over the world.

What must we do? God has said to me "Protect the Children," and as I get further and further into what that looks like I battle discouragement. My only answer is a book. That is a very passive answer. What action do I, one person, have to offer? If I join a Christian agency's efforts how will that be anything other than a drop in a bucket of need?

I still believe in giving them the only power out there that is able to defeat the enemy of their very life. Jesus told His disciples that the power from on high, Holy Spirit, was and is the answer. FIRE POWER!

United States

Main article: Human trafficking in the United States

In 2002, Derek Ellerman and Katherine Chon founded a non-government organization called the Polaris Project to combat human trafficking. In 2007, Polaris instituted the National Human Trafficking Resource Center (NHTRC) where[43] callers can report tips and receive information on human trafficking.[44] Polaris' website and hotline informs the public about where cases of suspected human trafficking have occurred within the United States. The website records calls on a map.[45]

In 2007, the U.S. Senate designated 11 January as a National Day of Human Trafficking Awareness in an effort to raise consciousness about this global, national and local issue.[46] In 2010, 2011, 2012 and 2013, President Barack Obama proclaimed January as National Slavery and Human Trafficking Prevention Month.[47] Along with these initiatives, libraries across the United States began to contribute to human trafficking awareness. Slowly, libraries turned into educational centers for those who are not aware of this issue. Libraries have also collaborated with organizations to train staff

A world map showing the legislative situation in different countries to prevent female trafficking as of 2009 according to *WomanStats Project*.
- Gray: No data
- Green: Trafficking is illegal and rare
- Yellow: Trafficking is illegal but problems still exist
- Purple: Trafficking is illegal but is still practiced
- Blue: Trafficking is limitedly illegal and is practiced
- Red: Trafficking is not illegal and is commonly practiced[32]

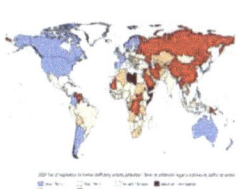

Findings of the legislative framework in place in different countries to prevent/reduce human trafficking. The findings are from the 2019 Department of State Trafficking in Persons Report[126]
- Blue – Tier 1
- Yellow – Tier 2
- Orange – Tier 2½
- Red – Tier 3
- Brown – Tier special

Source: https://en.m.wikipedia.org/wiki/List_of_organizations_that_combat_human_trafficking

133

Chapter 16 - Baby Baptism

The Wikipedia article on Infant Baptism states the following:

> *Scholars disagree on the date when infant baptism was first practiced. Some believe that 1st-century Christians did not practice it, noting the lack of any explicit evidence of paedobaptism. Others, noting the lack of any explicit evidence of exclusion of paedobaptism, believe that they did, understanding biblical references to individuals "and [her] household" being baptized (Acts 16:15, Acts 16:31–33, 1 Corinthians 1:16) as including young children.*
>
> *The earliest extra-biblical directions for baptism, which occur in the Didache (c. 100), are taken to be about baptism of adults, since they require fasting by the person to be baptized. However, inscriptions dating back to the 2nd century which refer to young children as "children of God" may indicate that Christians customarily baptized infants too. The earliest reference to infant baptism was by Irenaeus (c. 130– 202) in his work Against Heresies. Due to its reference to Eleutherus as the current bishop of Rome, the work is usually dated c. 180. Irenaeus speaks of children being "born again to God." This reference has been described as "obscure." Three passages by Origen*

(185–c. 254) mention infant baptism as traditional and customary. While Tertullian writing c. 198–203 advises the postponement of baptism of little children and the unmarried, he mentions that it was customary to baptize infants, with sponsors speaking on their behalf. The Apostolic Tradition, sometimes attributed to Hippolytus of Rome (died 235), describes how to perform the ceremony of baptism; it states that children were baptized first, and if any of them could not answer for themselves, their parents or someone else from their family was to answer for them.

From at least the 3rd century onward Christians baptized infants as standard practice, although some preferred to postpone baptism until late in life, so as to ensure forgiveness for all their preceding sins.

In the defense of baby baptism, the Gospel Coalition has written an article on its website: https://www.thegospelcoalition.org/blogs/kevin-deyoung/a-brief-defense-of-infant-baptism/
Most of the apologetics are from promises made to Abraham.

Someone greater than Abraham has come, Christ Jesus, the Son of God. In the book of Luke, Mary's encounter with Elizabeth in her 6th month of pregnancy is what I believe to be our example to follow. That was an act of power, dunamis power, which is also called virtue. Even in Jesus's ministry he touched the infants, unborn babes and children, imparting or transferring Holy Spirit and FIRE.

It is going to take more than what we have already known to do. Jesus brought Holy Spirit power to the babes in the womb, the infants and the children, with only a touch.

Our children are being stolen. Their minds are the target of the enemy when they are old enough to reason for themselves and in some cases even while very young. Christian children are taught songs and scripture and committed to the care of their church family to be raised up in the admonition of the Lord and even water baptized. Yet, they still can be lured away through vain philosophies.

Infants and toddlers are at the mercy of unbelieving parents and they are sold or even stolen, bought and sold for profit. Young virgins are stolen and sold, male and female.

The article at the beginning of this chapter is the process of baptism my Christian parent provided for me in good faith, trusting that it was a seal of protection unto God.

I grew up in a Christian home, went to public schools all my life, and left the church, which I called "the country club," by the time I graduated from high School. Water baptism and all the programs and personal scripture memorizing did not protect me from the vain philosophies of this world. I needed relationship, not knowledge. I needed to know I was loved, that I had a purpose and destiny, but I only knew the words about those things.

I left the church and the God of the Church. When I returned it took a major event to get me back at the door of the church and the Love of God to open it. From the age of 27 I was a Spirit-filled believer. People saw tongues of FIRE on my head, and I got water baptized again with understanding. I was baptized in The Holy Spirit at the age of 27. I'm 72 now, and in all that time no one was able to steal my faith in My Lord Jesus. I have come to Love Him and My Father, and Holy Spirit, my companion in this life.

And I know I'm not the only one who left their Christian upbringing. The prayers of the righteous, grandfathers, grandmothers, and moms and dads, make a difference in the trajectory of an individual's life in Christ.

But what if, instead of all the rescue ministries for the unborn babies, the children, the youth, we empower them from the very beginning with the same power John received in Elizabeth's womb? When Mary's voice was heard, John leaped in Elizabeth's womb and she was filled with the Holy Spirit. So the same Spirit that impregnated Mary and filled Jesus was able to transfer by sound, the power of the Holy Spirit to both Elizabeth and the baby in Elizabeth's womb. It was the FIRE that John the Baptist later declared when he said, "I baptize with water, but one is coming after me…who baptizes with

Holy Spirit and with FIRE."

No one ever took away John's faith. A foolish, drunk, Roman ruler took his life, but never his faith. John fulfilled his purpose on earth and returned to the Father victorious in death.

So, my point is, baptize babies in the Holy Spirit in the womb. That is the very power Jesus told His disciples to wait for, "the promise of the Father from on high," and then GO, make disciples.

The Scriptures show that without the power the going could not be accomplished. I believe we are in a time when only the FIRE Power of God can make a difference in the trajectory of the world.

Water baptism is the act of burying the old man in death, never to rise again. That is the decision that each individual will make for themselves. This is an earth decision. Flesh is temporary, and when it is discovered to be a detriment to each one, they will lay it down so the fullness of the Holy Spirit life can flow and the Kingdom FIRE can purify, illuminate, invigorate, penetrate, and assimilate to the image of God.

Holy Spirit baptism is a Kingdom decision. It is a promise of the Father for the power necessary for purpose and life on earth. Only God can protect His children. He pointed that out in ***Deuteronomy 32***. So let's get His protection in each baby so their life cannot be stolen by the enemy of God. I think the purifying work of the Holy Spirit FIRE begins even in the womb. Jesus has already paid their way.

Chapter 17 – Apologetics
By John A. Mapp, Jr.

One critically important aspect of protecting our children involves protecting their minds from the large number of bad ideas that have haunted each generation of human beings, up to and including the present time. It is incumbent on parents not only to teach Christian beliefs and values to their children, but also to arm them with information on these bad ideas in order to inoculate them and give them immunity. In order to do this, the parents themselves must first acquire the necessary information and skill to combat these ideas. This sounds like a daunting task, but there are some resources out there that can help.

One of these resources is a book entitled "Mama Bear Apologetics," edited by Hillary Morgan Ferrer. It is a very informative collection of essays written by moms, for moms. Ferrer, the primary author, starts out with a call to action for "mama bears" to rise up and face the challenges arrayed against Christian parents trying to raise their children in the Christian faith.

One key chapter, entitled "Linguistic Theft," describes how the English language is being subverted, with the definitions of words being changed to such an extent as to render them unrecognizable – and then being used against us like so many drones flying under the radar, but in this case evading detection through the mimicry of their former meanings. Examples include "love," "truth," "tolerance," and "justice."

Another chapter, entitled "My Brain Is Trustworthy…According to My Brain," explains the pitfalls of naturalism. The chapter is agreeably nuanced, as it lays bare the erroneous philosophical foundation of purely materialistic naturalism while at the same time recognizing the valid contributions of science along with the capacity of science and religion to peacefully coexist.

Another chapter, entitled, "The Truth Is, There Is No Truth," reveals how the philosophy of Postmodernism lacks even the intellectual coherence of naturalism by denying that there is any such thing as absolute truth. Postmodernists instead tend to see truth claims as power plays and techniques for perpetuating dominance. This school of thought has most especially flourished in colleges and universities, where the result has been the cultivation of disdain for western literature, culture, etc., along with the ideas that caused western civilization to flourish and yield unprecedented levels of freedom and prosperity for all of its inhabitants. Indeed, it has resulted in contempt for western civilization itself.

In the chapters that follow, Ferrer and her associates continue to tackle one challenge to Christianity after another, including radical skepticism, moral relativism, emotionalism, pluralism, feminism, Marxism, and even "progressive" Christianity.

The chapter on Marxism is particularly important and illuminating. However, I believe it leaves a lot unsaid that needs to be said. In the book's defense, it was published in 2019, and much has happened in just two short years since its publication. To fill in some of the gaps, I would like to offer some updated commentary in the pages that follow.

Marxism, it seems, evolves. Perhaps the most toxic form of Marxism currently in existence is called Critical Social Justice Theory (CSJT). CSJT includes (but is not limited to) critical theories involving race, gender, body type, and sexual orientation. The "Mama Bear" book does deal with a number of components and antecedents of CSJT (particularly Marxism and postmodernism), but not with the CSJT movement as a whole. This movement, or lens employed to look at contemporary challenges that we face, is so toxic that it rises to the level of an existential threat to our civilization. Moreover, the purveyors of these ideas have made it a priority to go after our children.

Since Marxism is most predominantly at the root of CSJT, some background is in order.

The harsh, punitive settlement imposed on Germany after the Great War (now known as World War I), along with the economic turmoil that followed, made Germany ripe for a totalitarian take-over starting in the 1920's. Two groups vied for control: The Marxists and the Nazis. In the 1930's, the Nazis won out, forcing the Marxists to flee the country. An influential group of Marxists emigrated to the United States, where they founded what became known as the Frankfurt School.

As the Frankfurt School and its philosophical descendants observed the increasing prosperity of workers in capitalist countries, along with the failure of orthodox Marxist countries to thrive, they recognized that there was a problem with their philosophy. Did they abandon Marxism? No – that would have made too much sense. Instead, they took the underlying principles of Marxism, consisting primarily of dividing people into oppressor and oppressed groups while making the alleged oppressed groups miserable, and applied it to other parameters besides social class. Hence, they began to cook up theories that divided people into opposing groups based on race, sex, sexual orientation, etc.

Think of it this way: Traditional Marxism was based on dividing people into oppressor and oppressed groups based on economic class (proletariat, or working class, versus bourgeoisie, or middle class). Traditional Marxism was like a mind virus that may be likened to a coronavirus. What the Frankfurt School did was like performing gain-of-function research on Marxism. When the Wuhan Institute of Virology did this with coronaviruses, the COVID-19 virus was the likely result. When the Frankfurt School did this with

Marxism, the result became known as Critical Theory.

Critical Theory, like its orthodox Marxist predecessor, operates dialectically according to ideas first formulated by the early nineteenth century German philosopher G. W. F. Hegel. The basic idea behind dialectical thinking was to start with a currently operational idea (the thesis) and confront it with its opposite (the antithesis). The outcome of this clash of ideas (the synthesis) would then become the new thesis. Hegel's dialectic existed in the realm of ideas. Karl Marx started with Hegel's dialectic and formulated an atheistic (yet still very much faith-based) philosophy that he called dialectical materialism. The dialectical materialism of Karl Marx held that repeated cycles of thesis – antithesis – synthesis formed a sort of arc of history that would ultimately result in a system he called communism. Marx believed that we were in the final phase of this historical push toward communism, and that capitalism was the thesis, socialism (under the dictatorship of the proletariat) was the antithesis, and communism would be the synthesis, or outcome.

Marxists believed in the inevitability of this arc of history, yet they also believed it their duty to hasten it to fruition by using every means at their disposal to make the proletariat, or working class, miserable with their current situation so that they would revolt and bring about socialism, thus hastening the path to communism. To put it bluntly, Marxism deliberately seeks to promote "wound collecting" (intentionally seeking and amassing historical grievances in a way that is toxic), thus cultivating a spirit of offense.

Critical Theories, the result of the Frankfurt School's gain-of-function research on Marxism, kept this same basic scheme but made it possible to divide people according to literally any parameter that the sin-enfeebled natural human mind could conceive of, be it race, sex, sexual orientation, body type, disability status, etc. The result is that, in this day and age, anyone whose mind is captured by one or more of these critical theories can become offended by literally anything that they put their minds to. Moreover, when they look at the world through the related additional lens of "intersectionality," they can locate themselves in multiple "oppressed" groups at once and thus feel even more thoroughly miserable and entitled, and thus become even more thoroughly deranged.

Thus, despite the fall of the Berlin Wall 32 years ago and the dissolution of the Soviet Union 30 years ago, and despite the obvious failure of orthodox Marxism wherever it has been tried, the basic ideas behind Marxism are as popular as ever.

Critical theories have been quietly inserting themselves into our institutions for decades. At this writing, (2021), they have recently been turbocharged by a handful of tragic and unfortunate incidents that reflect the messy world we live in. Thus, the quasi-religious critical theory ideologies, also referred to as "Cultural Marxism" or "Identity Marxism," have entered into a manic phase that is characterized by a kind of swarming behavior, or social contagion. As a result, the Critical Theorists have gained hegemony in a broad swath of our higher educational institutions, governmental organizations, news media, entertainment industry, tech companies, corporate HR departments, foundations and nonprofits, and even K-12 education, along with some school boards. A prime example of this swarming behavior includes all manner of mob action (both online and in real life) with the intent to shut down or "cancel" the objects of their ire, whether it be contemporary expressions deemed to be "wrongthink," cultural works deemed to be insufficiently "woke," or historical figures deemed to be "on the wrong side of history." People caught up in this type of thinking tend to take a dim view of individual liberties and rights, and are aggressively targeting our children with the intent of turning them from the Christian beliefs of their parents and convert them into "social justice warriors." The mobs have been working in and around captured institutions, which have allowed them to operate largely without restraint.

What is a parent to do?

We have to recognize that much conventional wisdom regarding preparing children to live in the world no longer applies. Many parents are still on autopilot. They think that they can trust the school system (whether public or private) to teach their children what they need to succeed in life. Many Christian parents think that their church's Sunday school and youth programs will adequately teach their children to remain in the Christian faith when they grow up. They also think that a college degree is a needed credential for a good job, and that what colleges teach is beneficial.

These beliefs may have been true once, but now that is no longer the case. In our current era, these business-as-usual, autopilot notions will do nothing but set up our children to fail, and set up our society and our very freedoms to fail with it.

My call to action is this: Parents must pivot aggressively and pursue new strategies. Parents must scrutinize what the schools teach their children, and show up at the school board meetings to speak out against toxic, divisive teachings and indoctrination. If the school system cannot be reformed, meaning it cannot be pried loose from the grip of woke idealogues, parents should withdraw their children from the system and homeschool them. Parents must diligently mentor their children in order to durably pass on their Christian beliefs. This includes not only warning their children about the most widespread alternative belief systems that children will encounter in their higher education, but also addressing more immediate challenges that will come through their friends and through the Internet. Parents need to stop viewing colleges and universities as mandatory, but rather should also be open to other ways through which children can be prepared to earn a living in life. These ways include trade schools, apprenticeships, and other practical forms of preparation.

Finally, to return to the main point of this book, it is not enough for children to be taught Bible stories, or simply to be taught **about** Jesus; they must be taught to know Jesus personally. This starts by guiding them into the born-again experience by encouraging children at an early age to trust Jesus for their salvation. But it does not stop there. Children should be taught about the *"Promise of the Father"* **(Luke 24:49)**. They should be led to ask God for the release of the power of the Holy Spirit in their lives. The Holy Spirit will *"guide them into to all the truth"* **(John 16:13)**. Armed with this power from on high, and reinforced by the prayers of the parents and grandparents, children will know instinctively to accept truth and reject error even when they encounter beliefs or situations for which they were not explicitly prepared.

Parents who do their due diligence by preparing their children for life in a way that takes into account the hazards of the current dark age in which we live, plus guiding them toward a personal relationship with Jesus Christ operating in the power of the Holy Spirit, will have well and truly prepared their children not only to take their rightful places in a dangerous world, but also to promote the world's redemption by reintroducing the Kingdom of God into the world.

Chapter 18 - Treasure of Great Worth

"Treasure of Great Worth" has been a long-time connection in my heart with the children of the AIDS infected regions of Africa.

Some years ago, I watched an Oprah Winfrey episode featuring her visit to a region in Africa to bring gifts to the children of AIDS victims. She was given permission by the leaders of the region, and had the help of volunteers from NATO and other organizations.

She had permission from one of the mothers that was dying of AIDS to interview her daughter. Oprah was invited into the shack/home of the little girl who was now in charge of her mother's care and her siblings.

Many children in the region were orphaned by the AIDS epidemic. Some of the young boys had been taken to become militia soldiers.

This little girl stood tall and spoke with confidence. Her goal was to go to school and become a doctor and cure the AIDS virus. Her confidence carried a spiritual weight. It went right into my heart and I believe Oprah felt the same thing. She caught her breath.

At that moment this thought came into my mind: Treasures of Great Worth are in these children and we must help them bring out the treasure. As the diamond must endure great pressure to be formed and gold must endure great heat to be refined and beautiful, these children have been pressed down and gone through the fires of life. These earthen vessels carry great treasure that God has hidden for their generation and the next and for His Glory.

I was reminded of the treasure in these children some years later when I did a demonstration in a Sunday school class on "Praying in Color." Not only did the children have treasure hidden, but the land did too, which I discovered in the activation.

Before I go on, let me introduce the author. It was begun by the wife of a Methodist pastor, Sybil MacBeth, to help children and adults who feel inadequate to put words to the prayers in their heart for family and friends. You just use a color or symbol or doodle to represent a person, situation, need, or other and say "God this is _____." Then you trust that God hears and understands, which of course He does.

So in my class that morning were three retired African missionaries from AIM, African Inland Mission. As the demonstration continued, I decided to draw the continent of Africa, as well as I could remember and then all of a sudden, I saw a band of the bluest water flowing from east to west over the nations of Egypt and Sudan on the east to Morocco, Algeria and Mauritania on the west, so I drew it on my paper and showed it to the missionaries.

They just looked at me and said that happened to be the region of the Sahara Desert. So my prayer was that the water that was hidden deep below the desert would become available to the people of Africa. This is the hidden treasure held deep in the land that must be excavated, like the treasure in the hearts of the children.

Another connection with Africa was in the 1980's. I met Dr. Nicku Mordi at ORU in Tulsa Oklahoma. We both had interesting stories of our arrival at ORU – a bit on the "amazing-hand-of-God-side" stories. We became friends for a short time only because I left the program before I graduated and Nicku went on to complete her doctorate.

Now, some 30+ years since that first meeting, we have reconnected. She put a message on Facebook asking friends from ORU to reconnect and my husband saw the message and gave me her info. We have reconnected and she has shared more of her personal story in the books she has written which give insight into the hand of God on her since she was a little girl, and on her children, as mentioned in the beginning of chapter 12.

Looking back on the generations of which we have first-hand information, we can see that many had treasure inside, hidden by the hand of God, to be discovered in each generation, and the hidden treasure must be discovered.

I believe the FIRE that John the Baptist spoke of is the missing ingredient of that awesome anointing needed to bring the power of God into every problem and situation in the world today and protect the children. Fire also can reveal the treasure that is hidden in each child.

I know throughout this entire book I have tried to point out the missing ingredient that God has already provided that can and will protect the children – The power or "FIRE" of the Holy Spirit.

But let's get real. There is more to it. These children really are treasures. The following is an excerpt from a teaching, presented by my friend and travel companion on the Kings Highway, Sharon Ahrens:

> CHRIST IN YOU IS THE TREASURE OF GREAT WORTH.
>
> *The Spirit within, is John's ever Flowing River, the Psalmist's Solid Rock, and Isaiah's, Great Shining Light. Finally, we understand that the in-dwelling Christ is the Treasure of Great Worth.*
>
> **2 CORINTHIANS 4:7** *"BUT WE HAVE THIS* **TREASURE** *IN EARTHEN VESSELS THAT THE EXCELLENCY (PREEMINENCE) OF THE POWER (DUNAMIS - ABILITY) MAY BE OF GOD, AND NOT OF US."*
>
> *The Greek word for "TREASURE" is "thesaurus," and it means, "a deposit, wealth; the place of safekeeping in which*

good and precious things are collected and laid up; a casket, a coffer, or other receptacle, in which valuables are kept; a treasury, storehouse, repository, or magazine; collected treasure." It is also used to speak of the Magi who opened their "TREASURES" for King Jesus. May we too, wisely present HIM with:

1. *Gold - the PRICE of a lifestyle of worship.*
2. *Frankincense - the PURITY (Innocence) of the lifestyle of worship.*
3. *Myrrh - the PAIN of the lifestyle of worship.*

The Bible explains that this treasure house beats in our chest - this TREASURE is your HEART.

My husband found these class notes in a stack of papers I was recycling and brought them to me saying, "Are you sure you want to discard this?" I have trusted The Lord to lead me through this entire writing so maybe HE was telling me something I couldn't yet see.

Sure enough, it's now my title and closing statement.

It's still about "Protecting the Children" and Holy Spirit, is that FIRE power for us and to us. Their hearts are on FIRE for God from the very first thought HE has of them. They arrive in time according to His Will and purpose, so let's give them a "winning chance to fly." I believe Mary, the mother of Jesus, was the first to protect the children in the FIRE power of the Holy Spirit. When she greeted Elizabeth, Elizabeth was filled with Holy Spirit FIRE, and so was John. He was in her womb.

Mary is our example to follow. We who have Holy Spirit FIRE speak in the authority of Jesus Christ to ignite what God has put in each one.

This is the last point in the dream to be uncovered. I believe what I just wrote is the revelation God gave me about the Dream. For every part of the Dream He has given me understanding. Many of the things I saw in the Dream were connected to things He showed me in the past. Now I am to take them off the shelf where they have waited for God's timing. And other parts are new revelation.

NOW IS THE TIME!

Appendix 1

Baby Book Example for Crafters

For Crafters -

1. An imagination-set-free
2. Blank board book - 6 X 6 - Available from Office Depot, Amazon, etc.
3. Stickers - Acid Free
4. Ink Pens - Acid Free
5. Pictures of Baby

ORDER OF BOARD PAGES

This little life

is a letter (a book)

of Christ written not with pen & ink

(2 Cor. 3:3) but with the Spirit of the living God.

Pg. 1-2	Pic / A gift from God sent our way / Psalm 127:3 NLT	Fearfully and wonderfully made. / Pic / Psalm 139:14	Pg. 9-10	Pic / and wisdom beyond his or her years / Matt. 11:25	and joy that brightens every room. / Pic / Neh. 8:10
Pg. 3-4	Pic / Light of the world / Eph. 5:8 Matt. 5:14	with purpose galore / Pic / Ex 9:16 Eph. 1:18-19 Eph 2:10	Pg. 11-12	Pic / Peace instead of fears / John 14:27 Psalm 121:7 Isaiah 41:10	Oh how loved you are. / Pic / John 1:12
Pg. 5-6	Pic / A blessing for all to see / James 1:17 Numb. 6:24-26	Kept safe in the Father's arms / Pic / Psalm 91:3-16			Treasured Productions
Pg. 7-8	Pic / Holy Spirit come. Fill this little one / John 3:8	with fire that can be seen. / Pic / Matt. 3:11			

Afterword: Other Dream and Final Word

It is September 8th, 4:30 am, and a dream awakens me, so I get up and start writing it down.

In my dream I was in the process of discovering some part of the original dream that led to the writing of my book. I was about to write it in my book when a voice called out to me.

"We found it. This way. The meaning of your dream is over here." I thought, "No it isn't. It's over here."

"It's my dream and I know what it means. You didn't have the dream, so how could you know what was given to me, in my head? Holy Spirit gave it to me to discover. I'm the author, you're just the publisher."

Then another thought entered my head. (I've recently found in some translations scripture that doesn't sound like The God I have come to know, and when I have investigated, sometimes I was right to question; and sometimes it was something I am yet to learn about God.) "What if the Bible had a publisher who 'corrected' the Spirit-filled writer's words because he didn't understand what was written and wanted to make it 'understandable' for the reader?"

Then it was as if The Lord began speaking to me, "The publisher found what was more easily understood by the reader. But the publisher did not find "WHAT I GAVE YOU."

All of a sudden, the heavens opened up and rain POURED DOWN outside. A major downpour was going on outside of my window. I smiled.

I believe that was a sign from God that I was thinking and hearing rightly. He was indeed speaking to me, specifically since it was rain coming down.

Years ago, when I lived in Houston Texas, HE was all I had. HE gave me *Isaiah 55*. It took me a number of years to understand what HE was saying to me. But what I really have solidly in my heart and mind are the verses that say,

> *"For as the rain comes down, and the snow from heaven, And do not return there, But water the earth, And make it bring forth and bud, That it may give seed to the sower And bread to the eater, So shall My word be that goes forth from My mouth; It shall not return to Me void, But it shall accomplish what I please, And it shall prosper in the thing for which I sent it. For you shall go out with joy, And be led out with peace; The mountains and the hills Shall break forth into singing before you, And all the trees of the field shall clap their hands"*
> *(Isaiah 55:10-12 NKJV).*

So once again as I am writing this in my book, it begins to pour down rain – A double confirmation. HE has given HIS Word to me to write this book. And whatever HE has sent it to accomplish it will accomplish. So be joyful and be led forth in peace, and listen – the mountains and the hills (of adversity) are going to break forth into singing before you. And others in The Garden of God will clap their hands.

Lord, I receive Your Word of promise and encouragement. AMEN

NOTE: This is a website I found while searching my Book title. It is an ebook written by a homeschooling mom that heard from God about children:
ttps://www.librariesofhopestore.com/uploads/6/3/0/0/63008883/achildsheart.pdf

What a wonderful journey I have been on. I feel like a king that has searched out the concealed treasures hidden by God. This treasure is in resemblance to FIRE, the ever present burning of the very Presence of God. And for His children it is the unending worship of the One who is worthy and the Power to live that life of worship to which they/we have been created to live.

The unfolding of how Jesus related to the children is the key to the message of this book, and the revelation brought to me in the discovery of the meaning of the Dream He gave me commanding me to "Protect the Children."

I'm closing this journey with a final statement, and a question.

The statement is in reference to the element of Fire used in the lives of many People groups throughout history. In many People groups, Fire was used for human sacrifice to their gods. Please, don't relate the FIRE of which I have written to be that kind of fire. Children sacrificed in the fire was the practice of those who worshipped Molech, the pagan god – A practice that was forbidden by the Hebrews and detestable to our God.

Now to the question. I have hinted, and, in some places, stated the possibility that we have forgotten something very necessary for a victorious life lived before our God: Becoming for Him His Ambassador of the Kingdom of which He is King, and will be once and for all King on the Earth.

He told us that the kingdom is like a little child, and we cannot enter the kingdom unless we become as a little child. He first encountered John in the womb of Elizabeth. Then later John said that Jesus was coming to baptize in Holy Spirit and FIRE. The scriptures revealed that the disciples didn't like people to bother Jesus with their children, but Jesus stopped them and said to permit it, "of such is the kingdom of God."

Not only did Jesus touch the children and bless the children, but I believe He blessed those who had not yet been born. Pregnant mothers came to Him and He blessed the child within them. Luke writes in six accounts of his gospel of the infants and unborn children. Luke was not one of the original disciples that had first-hand information, but he wrote what eye witnesses of Jesus's ministry told him. They saw the women and children of very small ages being brought to him.

The word that describes these unborn and small infants is G#1025. Check it out for yourself. So, could it be that when Jesus touched these children the same FIRE that John and Elizabeth received in His presence, they received? There was no water present. No dunking three times with scripture ceremonially spoken.

HE JUST TOUCHED THEM AND THE FIRE OF HOLY SPIRIT INFUSED THEM. They were secure in Him from the beginning of their lives. Filled with a heavenly power to accomplish on the earth that for which they had been created, just like Jesus. He was able to finish his work on earth.

Our works have been prepared for each and every one before the formation of this world, according the writer of the Ephesians epistle.

So, not knowing for sure, but believing I am to baptize babies with the FIRE of Holy Spirit, to obey God's call on my life, I will begin to seek out if this is what He has called me to and anointed me with His FIRE to give to the babes and small children. I will start with my own Grandchildren. They have not received any form of baptism, by some crazy circumstances. Maybe they have been waiting for the baptism of FIRE all along.

Since writing this Afterword I have had the opportunity to pray for Holy Spirit FIRE in four young adult males. When I Shared the main topic of my book with my friends, they wanted me to teach them how to pray for that FIRE for their children and grandchildren.

Bibliography

"2020 Trafficking in Persons Report." 2021. U.S. Department of State. https://www.state.gov/reports/2020-trafficking-in-persons-report/

Ahrens, Sharon. Christ the Treasure of Great Worth. *Teaching curriculum, 2010.*

Baucham Jr., Voddie T. Fault Lines: The Social Justice Movement and Evangelicalism's Looming Catastrophe. *Washington DC: Salem Books, an Imprint of Regnery Publishing, 2021.*

Clarke, Adam. Holy Bible with a Commentary and Critical Notes, Volume III, The Old Testament- Job to Solomon's Song. *New York: Abington-Cokesbury Press, 1977.*

Clarke, Adam. Holy Bible with a Commentary and Critical Notes, Volume V, The New Testament- Matthew to Acts, Page 53. *New York: Abington-Cokesbury Press, 1977.*

Ferrer, Hillary Morgan, General Editor. Mama Bear Apologetics: Empowering Your Kids to Challenge Cultural Lies. *Harvest House Publishers, 2020*

Hall, Verna. Christian History of the Constitution- Christian Self-Government, Volume I. *San Francisco, CA: Foundation for American Christian Education, 1972.*

MacBeth, Sybil. Praying In Color: Drawing a New Path to God. *Paraclete Press, 2007.*

Marshall, Perry. Evolution 2.0: Breaking the deadlock between Darwin and Design. *Dallas, Texas: BenBella Books, Inc., 2015*

"National Survivor Study." 2021. Polaris Project. https://polarisproject.org/national-survivor-study/.

Pillai, Bishop K. C., DD, Orientalism of the Bible, Volume 2, Proverbs chapters 1-16, Fairborn, Ohio, MOR-MAC Publishing Company, Inc. 1974

Pluckrose, Helen & Lindsay, James. Cynical Theories: How Activist Scholarship Made Everything about Race, Gender, and Identity – and Why This Harms Everybody. *Durham, NC: Pitchstone Publishing, 2020.*

Sartor, Jenna. Brave Part 1, *https://www.youtube.com/watch?v=-O7QEp4eEXE.*

Rose, James. The Short Course of American Christian History and Government. *Palo Cedro, CA: American Christian History Institute, 1994.*

Rosen, Jeffrey and Rubenstein, David. Essay: The Declaration, the Constitution, and the Bill of Rights. *(Accessed September 25, 2021)* https://constitutioncenter.org/interactive-constitution/white-papers/the-declaration-the-constitution-and-the-bill-of-rights?gclid=Cj0KCQjwkbuKBhDRARIsAALysV4RVNbnHRcn12DRXwjskDzGql7UzyOI_xWVj1hbgICp9ReaiCF3ZP8aAtsvEALw_wcB

Strong, James. The New Strong's Exhaustive Concordance of the Bible. *Nashville, TN: Thomas Nelson Publishers, 1990.*

Wikipedia, "Infant Baptism." Last modified 8 September 2021. https://en.wikipedia.org/wiki/Infant_baptism.

Wikipedia, "List of Organizations that Combat Human Trafficking." Last modified 14 September 2021. https://en.m.wikipedia.org/wiki/List_of_organizations_that_combat_human_trafficking.

Williams, Thomas. Knowing Aslan, An Encounter with the Lion of Narnia. *Nashville, TN: W Publishing Group, a Division of Thomas Nelson, 2005.*

Winfrey, Oprah, 20th Anniversary of the Oprah Winfrey Show, Set if 6 DVDs, 1 full length episode of her visit to South Africa where she gave gifts to 50,000 African Children. Produced by Harpo Studios.

The Author

For Sixteen years I was married to my job. That's what The Lord said to me when He called me away from the commercial design industry and sent me on my way to full time ministry, marriage and a family.

I could hear God laugh with delight when our first child was born when I was 40 years old and our second at 42. An Elizabeth or Sarah of the twenty first century. It was from this time forward our Children became "THIS ONE THING I DO" in my life. Feeling totally incapable of having the first idea about raising children, I began to read everything I could find. Actually, children scared me to death. There was something about them. I knew they could see straight into my soul. So, once I had my own, I wanted them to know they could trust me and I would do the best I could, and with the help of the Lord I would do better than I, alone, was able. And I wasn't alone. My husband was learning right alongside me. I discovered that God had put everything they would need for life and Godliness within each one, so all I had to do was help them become who God already knew them to be. He has every detail figured out and Holy Spirit is on task to make everything known, in God's time.

There is always more of God to know. He is unsearchable and Holy Spirit is the beloved messenger to the depths of God's love and the fullness of His understanding. This is what I wanted my children to have for life. And now I find there is even more for us from the depths of the Love of God, His Holy Spirit FIRE. It's His Kingdom FIRE.

Our children are grown and have families of their own. What I am learning is for them and their children, and even their children's children.

www.ingramcontent.com/pod-product-compliance
Lightning Source LLC
Chambersburg PA
CBHW070952180426
43194CB00042B/2343